Mathematical Programming Solver based on Local Search

FOCUS SERIES

Series Editor Narendra Jussien

Mathematical Programming Solver based on Local Search

Frédéric Gardi
Thierry Benoist
Julien Darlay
Bertrand Estellon
Romain Megel

WILEY

First published 2014 in Great Britain and the United States by ISTE Ltd and John Wiley & Sons, Inc.

ISTE Ltd
27-37 St George's Road
London SW19 4EU
UK

www.iste.co.uk

John Wiley & Sons, Inc.
111 River Street
Hoboken, NJ 07030
USA

www.wiley.com

Library of Congress Control Number: 2014936489

British Library Cataloguing-in-Publication Data
A CIP record for this book is available from the British Library
ISSN 2051-2481 (Print)
ISSN 2051-249X (Online)
ISBN 978-1-84821-686-0

MIX
Paper from
responsible sources
FSC® C013604
www.fsc.org

Printed and bound by CPI Group (UK) Ltd, Croydon, CR0 4YY

Contents

Acknowledgments

This monograph was originally written as Frédéric Gardi's Habilitation Thesis in Computer Science, publicly defended on November 25th 2013 at Université Pierre et Marie Curie (Paris, France) before a jury consisting of: Philippe Baptiste, Strategy & Innovation Director, MESR/DGRI (examiner); Yves Caseau, Executive Vice President, Bouygues Telecom (examiner); Philippe Chrétienne, Professor, Université Pierre et Marie Curie (president); Gérard Cornuéjols, Professor, Carnegie Mellon University (examiner); Michel Gendreau, Professor, École Polytechnique de Montréal (referee); Jin-Kao Hao, Professor, Université d'Angers (referee); Geir Hasle, Chief Research Scientist, SINTEF ICT (referee); and Marc Sevaux, Professor, Université de Bretagne-Sud (examiner). Nevertheless, the research advances presented in this monograph emerged from a collective work by the LocalSolver[1] team: Thierry Benoist, Julien Darlay, Bertrand Estellon, Frédéric Gardi, and Romain Megel. The authors thank Antoine Jeanjean, Karim Nouioua and Guillaume Rochart who contributed to part of the work presented here, as well as Thibaud Cavin, Lucile Robin, Saul Pedraza

---

1 http://www.localsolver.com.

Morales, Sofia Zaourar, Boris Prodhomme and Clément Pajean who worked with us as interns on related topics.

To our families and friends

Preface

This book deals with *local search for combinatorial optimization* and its extension to mixed-variable optimization. Our goal is to present local search in a new light. Although not yet understood from the theoretical point of view, local search is the paradigm of choice for tackling large-scale real-life optimization problems. Today, end users ask for interactivity with decision support systems. For optimization software, it means obtaining good-quality solutions quickly. Fast iterative improvement methods, such as local search, are suitable to satisfy such needs.

When a solution space is gigantic, a complete search becomes impractical. Given a (possibly infeasible) solution to the problem, local search consists of modifying some parts of this one – that is, some decision variables – to reach a new, hopefully better solution. Exploring a so-called *neighborhood* of the incumbent has a major advantage: the new solution can be evaluated quickly through *incremental calculation*. Then, local search can be viewed as an incomplete and non-deterministic but efficient way to explore a solution space.

First, an iconoclast *methodology* is presented to design and engineer local search algorithms. We show that the performance of a local search mainly relies on the richness of the neighborhoods explored, as well as on the efficiency of their exploration. Ultimately, implementing high-performance local search algorithms is a matter of expertise in *incremental algorithmics* and of dexterity in computer programming. Our concern to *industrialize* local search approaches will be of particular interest for practitioners. As an example, this methodology is applied to solve two industrial problems with high economic stakes.

Nevertheless, software applications based on local search induce extra costs in development and maintenance in comparison with the direct use of mixed-integer linear programming solvers. We present the *LocalSolver project* whose goal is to offer the power of local search through a model-and-run solver for *large-scale 0–1 nonlinear programming*. Having outlined its modeling formalism, the main ideas on which LocalSolver relies are described and some benchmarks are presented to assess its performance. We conclude the book by presenting our ongoing and future works on LocalSolver *toward a full mathematical programming solver based on neighborhood search*.

Frédéric Gardi
April 2014

Introduction

In this book, we present a survey of our research on local search in combinatorial optimization, from methodological foundations to industrial applications and software. This survey puts into perspective the evolution of our research, from the resolution of specific problems to the design of a general-purpose mathematical programming solver based on local search, namely LocalSolver. After a brief introduction about combinatorial optimization and local search, we outline the book's plan.

I.1. Local search in combinatorial optimization

A *combinatorial optimization* problem is characterized by the discrete nature of its solution space. In very general mathematical terms, such a problem consists of optimizing (minimizing or maximizing) a function f over a finite set of solutions S. Many organizational problems arising in business and industry can be modeled in these terms. When the cardinality of S is gigantic, enumerating all the solutions of the space to find the best one is impossible within reasonable running times. A scientific field, namely combinatorial optimization, has grown in the last 50 years whose aim is to study this kind of problem and to provide practical algorithmic solutions to these problems.

Despite positive results, numerous combinatorial optimization problems remain difficult. Firstly, being difficult in the sense of complexity theory: it is unlikely that an algorithm exists solving any problem in worst-case polynomial time. Secondly, being difficult because many algorithms efficient according to the theory are not so efficient in practice: $O(n^3)$-time or even $O(n^2)$-time algorithms become unusable face to the actual needs. That is why a vast body of literature has grown around approximate algorithms, also called heuristics, which do not guarantee to output optimal solutions. It is in this context that *local search* is generally presented. Prior to being a heuristic approach, local search is an optimization paradigm, which is referred to as *iterative improvement* in the literature. This paradigm is widely used not only in combinatorial optimization but also in continuous optimization in different terms. Conceptually, the idea is simple and natural. Given a (possibly infeasible) solution to the problem, local search consists of modifying some parts of this – that is, some of the decision variables – to reach a new, hopefully better solution. Such a modification is generally called *move* or *transformation*. Exploring a so-called *neighborhood* of the incumbent has a major advantage: the quality of the new solution can be evaluated quickly through *incremental calculation*. Then, the local search can be viewed as an incomplete and non-deterministic but efficient way to explore a solution space, in contrast to complete search consisting of enumerating all solutions.

Local search appears hidden behind many textbook algorithms from the simplest algorithm, such as bubble sort, to more complex algorithms such as maximum flow or maximum matching algorithms (see [AAR 03] for more details). The simplex algorithm for linear programming is probably the most famous local search algorithm, as a pivoting-based combinatorial approach to a continuous optimization problem. It is also the best example of our little understanding of local search algorithms: widely used by practitioners because it is empirically efficient, but frustrating for theorists due to invariably pessimistic worst-case results. What a puzzling situation: despite being the star of mathematical programming, the simplex algorithm is not efficient according to the complexity theory. Now the situation is changing: dramatic progresses in the understanding of heuristic algorithms have been made during the last decade with the rise of smoothed complexity [SPI 04], providing us with, as the first striking result, an explanation of why the simplex algorithm usually takes polynomial time.

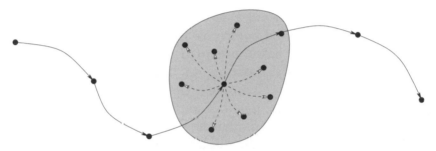

Figure I.1. *Local search = neighborhood search, that is, searching for better solutions in neighborhoods of an incumbent solution*

However, the concept of metaheuristics [GLO 86] – simulated annealing, tabu search, ant colony optimization, genetic algorithms, etc. [GLO 03] – has progressively supplanted the basic concept of local search. First published at the end of the 1990s, the survey by Aarts and Lenstra [AAR 03] was the first and last bestseller using the term "local search" in its title. Now, thousands of papers are being published each year presenting new metaheuristics, new applications of metaheuristics and comparisons of metaheuristics. A large number of these papers have poor technical content as well as a low practical impact [SÖR 12]. Unfortunately, this phenomenon has contributed to the idea that local search is not a way to make "serious" optimization, in particular among mathematicians.

I.2. Mathematical programming

There are different views of what is *mathematical programming*. In a broad sense, it can be seen as an old wording for mathematical optimization. On the other hand, mathematical programming also refers to the discipline concerned by the design of algebraic languages to *model* declaratively optimization problems, as well as by the design of general-purpose algorithms to *solve* these mathematical models. This discipline mixes both scientific and technological aspects: mathematics, computer science and software engineering. Nevertheless, our view of mathematical programming goes beyond this concept. Math programming software, usually called *solver*, is essentially built to serve people who need to solve *practical* optimization problems. This implies carefully listening to and understanding the needs of these people, who are generally referred to as *practitioners* or simply *users*. Common to all branches of applied mathematics, this latter aspect is critical to the success of the discipline: the dissemination of its outcomes in business and industry, and more generally in the whole of society.

Mathematical programming is divided into two main fields: *continuous optimization* and *discrete optimization*. Historically, these fields do not share much; they have different mathematical foundations, different algorithmic techniques, different application areas, and different scientific journals and conferences. Even though there is a trend in this direction, researchers and the practitioners are rarely involved in both fields. Linear programming can be viewed as the historical and scientific bridge between the two fields.

Continuous optimization, also called *numerical optimization*, is traditionally the domain of (applied) mathematicians. Applications of continuous optimization can be found in almost all branches of engineering: mechanics, design, process control, electricity, energy and finance. The algorithmic techniques used in continuous optimization mainly rely on iterative improvement based on derivatives – first- or second-order, exact or approximate – to guide the search (see [MIN 07]). Beyond linear programming, convex optimization has emerged as the largest class of problems for which efficient algorithms can be designed from both theoretical and practical points of view: interior point algorithms [BEN 01, WRI 04]. But in practice, approximating problems through accurate convex models is not always possible. Then, the development of non-convex programming solvers remains a hot topic. Several heuristic techniques have been designed to handle real-world nonlinear programs [LEY 10]: interior point methods, sequential linear and quadratic programming, augmented Lagrangian methods, or direct search, also known as derivative-free, methods. For more details on this topic, readers are advised to consult [BAZ 06, BEN 01, BON 00, KOL 03, MIN 07, NOC 06].

Combinatorial optimization is historically the field of operations researchers and computer scientists. Most of the applications can be found in management science: transportation and logistics, manufacturing, workforce scheduling and timetabling, network planning, etc. Tree search techniques – which consist of enumerating and pruning partial solutions, in particular by exploiting linear relaxations [COO 12] – are largely used by practitioners through mixed-integer linear programming solvers. Since many real-world problems are very large and highly combinatorial, heuristic techniques have been developed to provide good-quality solutions in reasonable running times. Iterative improvement techniques, such as local search, are particularly used in practice. Some attempts have been made to exploit direct local search approaches inside general-purpose solvers [ABR 99, CON 92, NON 98, RAN 01]. But to the best of our knowledge, no effective and widely used solver, based on the power of local search, has emerged so far. Nevertheless, tree search solvers integrate increasingly heuristic ingredients to speed up the search for good primal feasible solutions [LOD 13].

Until recently, mixed-variable optimization – involving both discrete and continuous decisions – was studied more by people working in combinatorial optimization. Mixed-variable nonlinear programming now becomes the focal point of the two communities. General-purpose solvers are now available to tackle this very general class of optimization problems, or some interesting subclasses such as mixed-integer convex quadratic problems. For recent surveys on techniques and software in this area, we refer the readers to [BEL 13, BUR 12, BUS 11, DAM 11]. However, these solvers are not widely used by practitioners since only small or specific problems can be efficiently addressed. Therefore, mixed-variable non-convex optimization appears as the next challenge in mathematical programming.

I.3. Outline of the book

This book deals with *local search for combinatorial optimization* and its extension to mixed-variable optimization. Our goal is to present local search in a new light. Although not yet understood from the theoretical point of view, local search is the paradigm of choice for tackling large-scale real-life optimization problems. Today, end users ask for interactivity with decision support systems. For optimization software, it means obtaining good-quality solutions quickly. Fast iterative improvement methods, such as local search, are suited to satisfy such needs.

First, an iconoclast *methodology* is presented to design and engineer local search algorithms. We show that the performance of a local search mainly relies on the richness of the neighborhoods explored, as well as on the efficiency of their exploration. Ultimately, implementing high-performance local search algorithms is a matter of expertise in *incremental algorithmics* and of dexterity in computer programming. Our concern to *industrialize* local search approaches will be of particular interest for practitioners. As an example, this methodology is applied to solve two industrial problems with high economic stakes.

Nevertheless, software based on local search induces extra costs in development and maintenance in comparison with the direct use of mixed-integer linear programming solvers. We present the *LocalSolver project* whose goal is to offer the power of local search through a model-and-run solver for *large-scale 0–1 nonlinear programming*. Having outlined its modeling formalism, the main ideas on which LocalSolver relies are described and some benchmarks are presented to assess its performance. We conclude the book by presenting our ongoing and future works on LocalSolver *toward a full mathematical programming solver based on local search*.

Local Search: Methodology and Industrial Applications

In this chapter, we present our methodology for tackling combinatorial or even mixed-variable optimization problems by local search. This methodology is designed to *industrialize* the engineering of local search heuristics, especially to solve large-scale combinatorial problems encountered in real-world situations. It may be viewed as iconoclast by some readers since it is not focused on "meta" aspects. In a sense, we advocate going back to basics. Having exposed this methodology, we illustrate it through two challenging industrial applications: car sequencing for painting and assembly lines (combinatorial optimization); vehicle and inventory routing (mixed-variable optimization).

1.1. Our methodology: back to basics

As presented in the introduction, local search is an iterative improvement technique that has been used by practitioners since the premises of combinatorial optimization. This is an approach of choice for tackling large-scale combinatorial problems, as encountered in the practice of operations research (OR). Unfortunately, we have no theoretical foundations yet that explain the good empirical results obtained by local search, contrasting with the bad behaviors predicted by worst-case studies. Then, local search is usually viewed as "cooking" by many practitioners and researchers. This view was considerably amplified with the rise of metaheuristics over the last 20 years. Mainly built on bio-inspired metaphors, the zoo of metaheuristics obscures local search today. This tendency can be observed not only in the literature related to combinatorial optimization, but also in its teaching and practice.

Many papers describing methodologies or good practices to engineer local search heuristics have been published. These methodological works are essentially concentrate on search strategies and more particularly on metaheuristics (see for example [HAN 08, LØK 07, PEL 07]): how to choose the good ones? How to tune them? We claim that this trend, namely "local search = metaheuristics", has resulted in bad engineering practices. Much time is spent in tuning parameters of metaheuristics. Worse still, much time is spent in trying different metaheuristics for the same problem. By increasing the cost of optimization software instead of lowering it, such practices go against the trend in information technology – better, faster and cheaper – and then against the spreading of OR in business and industry. If we get back to the seminal papers on local search, we can notice that the emphasis was not primarily put on the search strategy (now called metaheuristic), but more on the moves and their evaluation. For instance, a great part of the works done about the Lin–Kernighan heuristic for the traveling salesman problem concerns the speedup of the evaluation of the celebrated k-opt moves through incremental algorithmics.

Here we propose a methodology to design and engineer local search heuristics for combinatorial or mixed-variable optimization. Our goal is to provide a simple recipe to help practitioners deliver quality, fast, reliable and robust solutions to their clients, while lowering their development and maintenance costs as well as the risks on their optimization projects. This methodology is based on about 15 years of works in business, spent in solving real-life problems for operational users [BEN 09, EST 06, EST 08, EST 09, GAR 12, GAR 11, JEA 11]. The concrete nature of our experiments coupled with the business context was crucial in the design of this methodology: we insist on the fact that its purpose is to *industrialize the development of local search solutions for practical combinatorial optimization.*

1.1.1. *What are the needs in business and industry?*

After many years of OR practice, we have learnt important lessons about the needs of users in business and industry. First, clients have optimization problems, and rarely satisfaction problems. The "no solution found" answer is not an acceptable answer for end users. Indeed, they already have solutions in operations, even if these solutions may be bad (objectives poorly optimized, important constraints violated). Thus, once the optimization model is stated, finding a feasible solution should be easy. A good way to proceed is to adopt a *goal programming* approach [JON 10]: relaxing some constraints by introducing slack variables, then minimizing the violation of these constraints as primary objective. Even when a solution violating such "soft" constraints is unacceptable, seeing it is very useful for the user to detect the cause of the problem, which is almost always an inconsistency in input data.

Thus, optimal solutions are not what clients really want first. Proof of optimality is much less what they want. They want, first, nice and easy-to-use software providing good solutions quickly. Visualizing and modifying solutions, as well as interacting with the optimizer, is often more critical than the quality of results. Furthermore, clients are more sensitive to what we call local optimality. If the solution output by the optimizer can be improved by hand (generally by mimicking local search), then the clients surely consider this solution as bad. Surprisingly, this will be the case even if the original solution is close to a global optimum. However, optimal solutions are sometimes rejected because their structure is too far from the structures commonly known by the user, or just too complicated for him/her to understand. Ultimately, psychological aspects and change management are critical: if the end users do not understand and trust the solutions provided by the optimization software, they will not use it in the long run. Having completed dozens of optimization projects (to a greater or lesser extent successful), we can conclude that proving optimality or gaining the final percents in solution quality is insignificant in comparison with the relevance of the mathematical model, the accuracy of input data, the ergonomics of the whole software and its integration in the information system, as well as the project and change management. The interested reader is invited to consult our paper [BEN 11a] for more details on these non-scientific but crucial aspects in the practice of OR.

1.1.2. *The main ingredients of the recipe*

Our approach to local search is primarily *pure* and *direct*. No decomposition is done: the problem is tackled head on. The search space explored by our algorithm is close to (or even extends) the original solution space. In case of mixed-variable optimization, the combinatorial and continuous parts of the problem are treated together: combinatorial and continuous decisions can be simultaneously modified by a move during the search. By avoiding decompositions or reductions, no solution is lost and the probability of finding high-quality solutions is increased. To simplify the software design and then to facilitate maintenance, we avoid hybridization: no particular metaheuristic is used and no tree search technique is used. Then, our methodology is mainly focused on *designing rich neighborhoods ensuring an effective randomized exploration of the search space* and *speeding up the evaluation of these neighborhoods through incremental computation*.

Like any resolution approach, local search is sensitive to the way the solution space is designed. Since the main idea of local search is to move from one feasible solution to another by preferably modifying only a few decisions, the search space should be modeled to ensure that such moves can succeed with a high probability. The main cause of failure of a move is the presence of severe constraints in the optimization model: the neighbor reached through the move is infeasible with respect to these constraints. Therefore, local search is not suited to tackle tightly constrained problems. The more the search space is constrained, the larger the neighborhoods explored must be, in the hope of finding better feasible solutions. However, as explained previously, tightly constrained problems generally result from bad modeling practices. The other cause of failure is related to the combinatorial landscape induced by the objective optimized over the solution space [REI 02]. When the landscape is very rugged, many local optima are encountered during the search, requiring possibly uphill moves to escape them. However, when the landscape is very flat, the search may be lost over large plateaus (solutions with equal cost), slowing the convergence toward high-quality solutions. Rugged landscapes may result from numerical objectives involving many insignificant digits (which can be viewed as a kind of noise), while flat landscapes generally result from objectives inducing high combinatorial steps. Refining the optimization model to avoid such situations is generally fruitful for both solving and business purposes. Note that neutral walks [BAR 01] – moves along solutions with equal cost – also known as plateau searches [SEL 92], are a good way to diversify the search without uphill moves (see, for example, our work on the car sequencing problem [EST 06, EST 08] described in the next section).

Nevertheless, exploring large neighborhoods is the best way to diversify the search and ensure the convergence toward high-quality local optima. Since exploring such neighborhoods requires more running time, a trade-off between quality and efficiency has to be found. We propose to first explore *small but rich neighborhoods* in order to exploit the best invariants and thus benefit from *fast incremental evaluations* (generally running in constant time for each explored neighbor). In this way, a large number of solutions can be visited within the time limit, which becomes crucial when partially exploring a gigantic solution space: the more solutions you explore, the more chance you have of finding good ones.

1.1.3. *Enriching and enlarging neighborhoods*

A pragmatic way to proceed in practice is to design neighborhoods step by step – from the cheapest to the largest – as the need for quality solutions grow. It allows us to reduce the time to deliver the first solutions to the clients, which is critical to the success of real-world optimization projects [BEN 11a]. First, we advocate the use of a *large variety of small randomized moves*. The neighborhood of the incumbent corresponds to the set of solutions reachable through all possible moves. Denoting n as the size of the solution, the idea is to explore an $O(n^k)$-size neighborhood with small values for k (typically $k = 2$) but with a large constant hidden by the big O notation (see Figure 1.1). To speed up the search while avoiding bias or cycling phenomena, the neighborhood is explored following a *first-improvement fashion* (as soon as a better or equal solution is found, this one becomes the new incumbent) *coupled with randomization*. For example, for a machine scheduling problem, the following standard moves are commonly used: insert a task in the schedule, remove a task from the schedule, move a task in the schedule, swap two tasks of the schedule. These moves can be naturally generalized by considering a block of consecutive tasks and not only one task. If needed, we can go further. By designing larger and richer moves: sequentially move k blocks or cyclically exchange k blocks in the schedule. By designing more specific moves: select tasks randomly, select tasks on the same machine, select tasks on different machines, select tasks along the critical path, select tasks saturating some constraints. Adding more complex moves allows us to enlarge the explored neighborhood. Adding more specific moves allows us to concentrate the search on more promising parts of the whole neighborhood. In practice, these kinds of rich neighborhoods generally suffice to obtain high-quality solutions quickly: we present strong empirical evidences of this claim in the next sections, derived from our papers [BEN 09, EST 08].

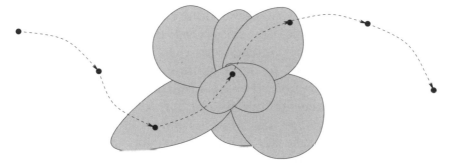

Figure 1.1. *Large neighborhood induced by the union of multiple small neighborhoods*

The first way to further enlarge the neighborhood explored is to use *compound moves*. The idea is simple: applying a number of small moves consecutively (or possibly following a backtracking scheme) to find a better feasible solution. The decisions modified at each step of the process are frozen to avoid cycling. This kind of neighborhood exploration allows us to jump along infeasible or uphill solutions during the search. This technique is related either to the Lin–Kernighan heuristic [HEL 00, HEL 09] or to the Ruin and Recreate heuristic [SCH 00] when the first move destroys the feasibility of the incumbent. Some applications of this kind of neighborhood are described in our papers [EST 09, GAR 11]. To go further still, one can explore *exponential-size neighborhoods*. The exploration can be performed using tree search techniques or efficient algorithms in some specific cases (through reduction to polynomial or pseudopolynomial problems). Such neighborhoods are very time-consuming to explore in comparison to small ones, which make them rarely useful in practice. An application of this kind of neighborhood as well as a discussion about their practical relevance can be found in our papers [EST 06, EST 08].

The idea of mixing neighborhoods having different structures and sizes to improve the quality of local optima is not new. This is the main idea behind the variable neighborhood search metaheuristic [HAN 08]. During the writing of this book, we discovered that Sörensen *et al.* [SÖR 08] recently introduced the term "multiple neighborhood search" to describe this approach, commonly encountered in commercial vehicle routing software. Here we detail some engineering ingredients that make a difference in practice. In particular, the systematic use of randomization during the search is critical for its diversification. Randomization limits the risk of omitting some promising regions of the search space. More generally, randomization helps in avoiding pathological worst-case behaviors.

1.1.4. *High-performance software engineering*

Incrementality is a core concept in local search. Let S be the current solution and S' the solution to evaluate in the neighborhood of S. Denote by $|S|$ (respectively $|S'|$) the length of S (respectively $|S'|$). Then, denote by Δ the "amount of change" between S and S'. For example, when optimizing a Boolean function, Δ represents the number of variables whose value is changing between S and S'. The part of S that remains unchanged in S' is called *invariant*. Evaluating S' incrementally consists of evaluating the cost of S' in a time smaller than $O(|S'|)$, hopefully in $O(\Delta)$ time. For more formal details about incremental computation, the interested reader is referred to [RAM 96]. In this way, the smaller the change from S to S', the faster the evaluation. In particular, if a move is such that Δ remains constant with respect to $|S|$ (that is, $\Delta \ll |S|$), then this move may be evaluated in constant time. Consequently, exploiting invariants helps us to speed up the convergence of local search by several orders of magnitude. Moreover, careful implementations – awareness of the locality principle ruling the cache memory allocation and optimized by code profiling [MOR 02a, MOR 02b, MOR 01] – still helps us to accelerate the search (see [ZHA 03] for some experiments on SAT solvers). Thus, it is not surprising to observe an order of 10 or even 100 between the times of convergence of two local search heuristics, apparently based on the same principles. Thus, refining search strategy or tuning metaheuristic parameters is irrelevant while the evaluation machinery is not well optimized. Our experience shows that the improvements in terms of solution quality brought by working on search strategy are negligible compared to improvements obtained by enriching the moves and speeding up the evaluation machinery. Ultimately, our local search heuristics are composed of three layers: the search strategy, the pool of moves inducing neighborhoods and the incremental evaluation machinery. The working time spent to engineer each layer during a project follows approximately this distribution: 10% for the search strategy, 30% for the moves and 60% for the evaluation machinery.

Linked to algorithmics, software engineering aspects such as reliability are no less crucial than efficiency. Local search is an iterative improvement approach relying on complex algorithms and data structures. Thus, engineering local search requires larger efforts in verification and testing than for common software. Consequently, the verification process of local search software has to be industrialized too. Here our best practices are summarized. The first one is to program with assertions [ROS 92]. It consists of verifying preconditions, postconditions and invariants throughout the program in order to validate each of its steps. Since formal verification remains expensive for basic software projects, the general idea behind programming with assertions is to check the results of a piece of code with a different piece of code. Such a practice reduces the number of coding errors drastically and thus the probability of software failures. Categorically, the consistency of all dynamic data structures – in particular the ones used for incremental evaluation of the moves – is checked after each iteration of the local search in debugging mode, by recomputing them from scratch using brute algorithms independent from the local search code. Consequently, a large part of the source code of our local search heuristics is dedicated to verification and testing: from experience, code checkers represent more than 10% of the whole source code. Hence, reliability aspects, as well as maintainability and portability issues, must be taken into account to carefully calculate the cost of optimization projects relying on local search.

1.2. Car sequencing for painting and assembly lines

The subject of the ROADEF 2005 Challenge[1] addressed a real-life car sequencing problem proposed by the French automotive company Renault. This problem consists of determining the order in which a set of vehicles should go inside the factory so as to make the whole process of fabrication easier: first, through the paint workshop where the car is painted, then along the assembly line where the equipment and options of each vehicle are set. For the paint workshop, the objective is to minimize the number of purges (or color changes), which amounts to group vehicles that have the same color. Nevertheless, the number of consecutive vehicles having the same color must not exceed a certain value, namely the paint limit. Then, in order to smooth the workload on the different stations composing the assembly line, it is necessary to space out the vehicles for which setting

---

1 http://challenge.roadef.org/2005/en.

options needs some heavy operations. This need of spacing out vehicles is formalized by defining a ratio for each option. For example, for an option to which the ratio 3/7 is associated, we hope to find no more than 3 vehicles requiring the option in any contiguous subsequence consisting of 7 vehicles (such subsequences are called windows). Then, the objective is to minimize the number of violations for all the ratios. In the previous example, if five vehicles have the option in a window of seven, then two violations are counted. Here the options are classified into two kinds: priority and non-priority. The objective function is composed of three terms that are minimized in lexicographic order: the number of color changes (RAF), the number of violations on priority options (EP) and the number of violations on non-priority options (ENP). Three kinds of objectives are possible: EP/ENP/RAF, EP/RAF/ENP and RAF/EP/ENP.

The car sequencing problem is strongly NP-hard, even if only options with ratio 1/2 are considered [EST 13]. The previous works on the subject [GOT 03, GRA 05, KIS 04, PUC 02, SOL 00] dealt only with the constraints and objectives related to the assembly line. The brute force use of integer or constraint programming software reaches its limit when 100 cars with few options are considered, while some instances with 1,000 cars have to be tackled. Then, several heuristic approaches have been proposed to solve the problem practically: greedy algorithms [GOT 03], ant colony optimization [GOT 03, GRA 05, SOL 00] and local search [GOT 03, PUC 02]. All these approaches have been intensively studied and experimented in the context of the ROADEF 2005 Challenge [SOL 08]. In effect, the heuristics designed by the different competitors to the challenge are essentially based on local search, integrated into different metaheuristic schemes. Moreover, several works have been done to hybridize local search and exact approaches such as constraint programming [PER 04a, PER 04b] or integer programming [EST 06, EST 08, PRA 08]. Our extensive works on this subject [EST 06, EST 08] show that exploring large neighborhoods through matching algorithms in addition to small moves leads to some improvements, but is negligible in comparison to the engineering efforts necessary to obtain them.

We outline a local search heuristic that enabled us to win the challenge in both junior and senior categories. The results obtained on the classical or Renault car sequencing problems remain the state-of-the-art. Our approach follows the methodology described above: a fast exploration of several small but rich neighborhoods. Our search strategy is simply a standard first-improvement descent. The main conclusion drawn from our victory is that sophisticated metaheuristics are useless in solving car sequencing problems. More generally, it demonstrates that algorithmic aspects, often neglected in favor of trendy "meta" aspects, remain the key ingredients for designing and engineering high-performance local search heuristics. For more details on this topic, the reader is referred to our papers [EST 06, EST 08].

1.2.1. *Search strategy and moves*

The initial solution is built using a greedy algorithm [EST 08, GOT 03]. We use a first-improvement standard descent as general heuristic. The algorithm applies a move to the current sequence at each iteration. The move is picked randomly in a pool of moves following a non-uniform distribution. The reader is referred to [EST 08] for more details about this distribution, which is not crucial outside a context of competition. If the move induces no violation on paint limit constraints and does not deteriorate the cost of the current solution, then this move is committed. Otherwise, it is rejected.

Four classical moves [GOT 03, PUC 02] are used: swap, forward insertion, backward insertion and reflection. A swap consists of exchanging the positions of two vehicles in the sequence. A forward insertion localized on a portion v_i, x, y, z, v_j of vehicles consists of extracting v_j, shifting the vehicles v_i, x, y, z to the right and reinserting v_j at the position that remains unfilled (the former position of v_i); after the move, the initial portion contains the vehicles v_j, v_i, x, y, z in order. A backward insertion is defined in a symmetric way, by extracting v_i instead of v_j. A reflection between two vehicles v_i and v_j consists of reversing the portion of vehicles between v_i and v_j.

There are $n(n - 1)/2$ combinations for choosing the positions, where to apply a move. Thus, the neighborhood explored through these moves is of size $O(n^2)$, with n being the number of cars to sequence. The selection of the neighbor is guided by no sophisticated rule: the first neighbor lowering or even equaling the cost of the current solution is retained for a new neighborhood exploration. Note that accepting the moves which do not strictly improve the cost (that is, neutral moves) is crucial. Coupled with a fast evaluation, this is a way to widely diversify the search [BAR 01, SEL 92].

1.2.2. *Enriching the moves and boosting their evaluation*

The simplest way to choose the positions to apply swaps, insertions or reflections consists of randomly picking the positions i and j. When numerous violations appear, such random moves are effective in minimizing the ratio objectives quickly. However, smarter strategies for choosing positions are useful when finding better solutions becomes difficult. More formally, this issue arises when finding an improving neighbor randomly in an $O(n^2)$-size neighborhood asks for $O(n^2)$ time. The idea is to reduce this running time by visiting neighbors (that is, by attempting moves) having a higher probability of success. Such a selection can be made without significant time overheads. These strategies depend on what the objective to optimize is and which kind of move is applied. For swaps, choosing vehicles sharing some options or having the same color naturally augments the chance of success of the move. In the same way, choosing adjacent positions in the sequence limits the risk of deterioration while making the evaluation faster. For insertions and reflections, a good strategy consists of choosing i and j, such that the distance $|j - i|$ is equal to the denominator of one of the ratios. When RAF is the prime objective, choosing the positions i and j as starting or ending point, respectively, of a sequence of vehicles having the same color limits the chances of breaking such sequences. All the strategies are detailed in [EST 08].

The bottleneck of each iteration of the local search in terms of time complexity is clearly the evaluation of the move that is attempted. Fortunately, almost all moves reveal some invariants that can be exploited using special data structures to evaluate the impact of a move on the cost of the current solution quickly. For ratios, the crucial remark is that the number of windows which are impacted by swaps, insertions or reflections depends only on the denominator of each ratio, generally small in practice. For swaps, only windows containing the two exchanged vehicles v_i and v_j are perturbed. In the case of insertions, the windows that are entirely contained between the vehicles v_i and v_j are just shifted by one position. Thus, only windows containing v_i and v_j must be considered for the evaluation of insertion moves. The same idea holds for reflections since windows entirely contained between extremal positions i and j are reversed, which leaves the number of violations into these ones unchanged. These remarks form the basis of the proofs of the following propositions [EST 08]. For any ratio P_k/Q_k, the number of windows impacted by a swap, an insertion or a reflection is at most $2\,Q_k$. Then, evaluating the new number of violations for this ratio following one of these moves can be done in $O(Q_k)$ time. Detecting some violations of paint limit constraints and evaluating the new number of purges following a swap, an insertion or a reflection can be done in $O(1)$ time.

Since there is no compensation between the objectives EP, ENP and RAF, the order of their evaluation is significant. In many cases, the evaluation process can be stopped before evaluating all the objectives. In the same way, starting the evaluation by checking if the move respects the paint limit constraints is judicious, since the verification takes only $O(1)$ time. The evaluation can be further improved heuristically for ratios. Indeed, the ordering in which the ratios are evaluated is significant. Suppose that having evaluated a move, the number of violations newly created for a subset of ratios is greater than the total number of violations for the remaining ratios (that are not evaluated yet). Even if the number of violations for the remaining ratios falls to zero, the move still deteriorates the sequence. Then, the evaluation can be stopped immediately and the move can be rejected. Accordingly, evaluating ratios following the decreasing order of the number of violations is a good heuristic for deciding earlier the rejection of the move. Since the evaluation of ratios is the most time-consuming routine, it still helps to reduce the practical running time of the local search.

1.2.3. *Experimental results and discussion*

Our local search heuristic was implemented in C programming language (4,000 lines of code). The running time was limited to 10 minutes on a standard computer by Renault. Our algorithm, ranked first, obtained the best result for almost all instances of the challenge. All the data, results and rankings can be found at http://challenge.roadef. org/2005/en or in papers [EST 08, SOL 08]. The algorithm greatly improved the results obtained by Renault, thanks to an apparently equivalent local search heuristic (simulated annealing coupled with swap moves) but without fast incremental computation. As a result of the competition,

Renault deployed our algorithm in its 17 plants worldwide, generating important annual savings.

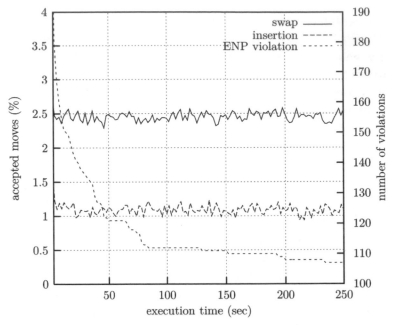

Figure 1.2. *Zoom of ENP optimization on instance 025-38-1-EP-ENP-RAF*

The number of attempted moves exceeds 150,000 per second, that is 100 millions over the 10 minutes of running time. Almost all these attempted moves are feasible. Here a feasible move means that its application results in a feasible solution (i.e. a feasible sequence of cars). This is due to the fact that constraints of the problem are not so hard to satisfy here, inducing a huge solution space. Thus, the diversification rate, namely the percentage of accepted moves (i.e. which are not rejected), varies between 1% and 10% according to the instances. For all instances, the percentage of accepted moves remains constant while the objective function is lowered (see Figure 1.2). Such a diversification rate, constant throughout the search thanks to neutral moves, allows us to diversify the search widely and, thus, explore many different regions of the solution space. This point is crucial for the effectiveness of any incomplete search algorithms, especially local search approaches.

Another interesting observation is that exploring larger neighborhoods is useless in this problem. Indeed, it is possible to explore exponential-size neighborhoods efficiently using (polynomial) flow or even assignment algorithms [EST 06, EST 08]. Even though they are customized and highly optimized [EST 06], such explorations bring no substantial improvement in solution quality as well as in convergence time, even for longer running times. Despite being polynomial, each exploration remains very time-consuming in comparison to the evaluation of small moves like swaps: 100 large moves versus 10 million small moves, per minute. Consequently, the expected running time to improve (the time spent to explore the neighborhood multiplied by the probability to find an improving solution) for these larger moves is several orders of magnitude higher than that for small moves. We can conclude that for the car sequencing problem, a basic search strategy coupled with small but enriched moves boosted by fast incremental evaluations is better than sophisticated search strategies, even if it is based on good mathematical properties (see propositions 3.1, 3.3 and 3.4 in [EST 06]).

1.3. Vehicle routing with inventory management

Vehicle routing with inventory management refers to the optimization of transportation costs for the replenishment of customers' inventories: based on consumption forecasts, the vendor organizes delivery routes. For the sake of concision, only the main features of the problem are outlined. A product is produced by the vendor's plants and consumed at customers' sites. Both plants and customers store the product in tanks. Reliable forecasts of consumption (respectively production) at the customers (respectively plants) are available over a discretized short-term horizon. The inventory of each customer must be replenished by tank trucks so as to never fall under its safety level. The transportation is performed by vehicles formed by coupling three kinds of heterogenous resources: drivers, tractors and trailers. Each resource is assigned to a depot. Now, a solution to the problem is given as a set of shifts. A shift is defined by: the depot (from which it starts and ends), the vehicle (driver, tractor and trailer), its starting date, its ending date and the chronologically ordered list of performed operations. Then, an operation is defined by the site where the operation takes place, the quantity delivered or loaded, its starting and ending dates. Thus, the inventory levels for customers, plants and trailers can be computed from the quantities delivered or loaded during the shifts.

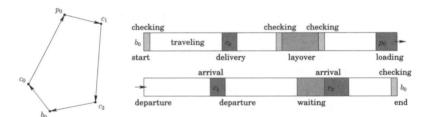

Figure 1.3. *Two views of the shift* $s = (b_0, c_0, p_0, c_1, c_2, b_0)$: *the route and the schedule*

The constraints on shifts are called *routing constraints*. A shift must start from the depot where the resources composing the vehicle are located, and must end by returning to this one. Some triplets of resources are not admissible. Each resource can be used during only one of its availability time windows. The working and driving times of drivers are limited; as soon as a maximum duration is reached, the driver must take a layover with a minimum duration. In addition, the duration of a shift cannot exceed a maximal value depending on the driver. The sites visited along the tour must be accessible to the resources composing the vehicle. The date of pickup/delivery must be contained in one of the opening time windows of the visited site. Two graphical views of a shift are illustrated in Figure 1.3.

Inventory constraints can be modeled as a flow network. Two kinds of inventories have to be managed: tanks of sites (customers and plants) and trailers. In any case, the quantity in storage must remain between zero and its capacity. For a customer c, the tank level $l(c, h)$ at each time step h is equal to the tank level at the previous time step $h - 1$, minus the forecasted consumption $F(c, h)$ over h, plus all the deliveries performed over h. The quantities delivered to customers must be positive (loading is forbidden at customers). Hence, the inventory dynamics at any time step h for customer c can be formally written as:

$$\begin{cases} l(c, h) = l(c, h - 1) - F(c, h) + \displaystyle\sum_{o \subset O(c,h)} q(o) \\ \text{if } l(c, h) < 0, \text{ then } l(c, h) = 0 \end{cases}$$

with $q(o)$ being the quantity delivered during an operation o and $O(c, h)$ being the set of operations performed at site c whose starting date belongs to time step h. Forbidding stockouts corresponds to force $l(c, h)$ to be greater than the safety level for each customer c and each time step h. Similar equations hold for plants whereas the inventory dynamics for trailers is much simpler since operations performed by a trailer cannot overlap. Hence the quantity in a trailer is not defined for each time step but after each of its operations. Starting at an initial level, this quantity is merely increased by loadings and decreased by deliveries.

The objective of the vendor over the long term is to minimize the total cost of shifts. The cost of a shift depends not only on the working duration and the distance traveled, but also on the number of deliveries, loadings and layovers appearing during the shift. This cost is usually divided by the total delivered quantity in order to increase the readability of this economic indicator. The cost per ton ratio (or miles per ton when costs are approximated by distances), namely the logistic ratio, is widely used in industry and in academic literature. Since reliable forecasts (for both plants and customers) are only available over a 15-day horizon, shifts are operationally planned day after day with a short-term rolling horizon of 15 days. It means that each day, a distribution plan is deterministically built for the next 15 days and shifts starting on the current day are fixed. Large-scale instances have to be tackled within short computing times. A geographic area can contain up to several hundred customers. All dates and durations are expressed in minutes and the inventory dynamics for plants and customers are computed with a time step of one hour. The execution time for computing short-term planning is limited to 5 mins on standard computers.

Following the methodology previously described, a new practical solution approach is presented for tackling this real-life inventory routing problem (IRP). This generalization of the vehicle routing problem was often handled in two stages in the past: first stage – inventory; second stage – routing. On the contrary, a characteristic of our local search approach is the absence of decomposition, made possible by a fast volume assignment algorithm. Moreover, thanks to a large variety of randomized neighborhoods, a standard first-improvement descent is used instead of tuned, complex metaheuristics. An extensive computational study shows that our solution provides long-term savings exceeding 20 % on average compared to solutions built by a classical urgency-based constructive algorithm or even by expert planners. Confirming the promised gains in operations, the resulting decision support system was deployed worldwide. For more details on this topic, the reader is referred to our paper [BEN 09].

1.3.1. *State-of-the-art*

Since the seminal work of [BEL 83] on a real-life IRP, a vast body of literature has emerged on the subject. In particular, a long series of papers was published by [CAM 98, CAM 02, CAM 04a, SAV 07, SAV 08], motivated by a real-life problem encountered in the industry. However, in many companies, inventory routing is still done by hand or supported by basic software, with rules like: serve emergency customers (that is, customers whose inventory is about to run out) using as many maximal deliveries as possible (that is, deliveries with quantity equal to the trailer capacity or, if not possible, to the customer tank capacity). For more references, the interested reader is referred to the recent papers by [SAV 07, SAV 08], which give a comprehensive survey of the research done on the IRP over the past 25 years.

To our knowledge, the sole papers describing practical solutions for such a broad IRP are the ones by Savelsbergh *et al.* [CAM 02, CAM 04c, SAV 07, SAV 08]. The approaches described in these papers are the same in essence: the short-term planning problem is decomposed to be solved in two phases. In the first phase, it is decided which customers are to be visited in the next few days, and a target amount of products to be delivered to these customers is set. In the second phase, vehicle routes are determined taking into account vehicle capacities, customer delivery windows, drivers' restrictions, etc. The first phase is solved heuristically by integer programming techniques, whereas the second phase is solved with specific insertion heuristics [CAM 04b].

1.3.2. *Search strategy and moves*

Following the methodology described above, when feasible solutions are not trivial to find or are even unlikely to exist, a good modeling practice is to relax some constraints by introducing appropriate penalties. In the present case, the no-stockout constraints are removed and a penalty is introduced, counting for each customer the number of time steps for which the quantity in tank is smaller than the safety level. This stage ensures that the software always returns a (possibly infeasible) solution. The initial solution is built using a classical urgency-based constructive algorithm. Then, the heuristic is divided into two optimization phases: the first one consists of minimizing the number of stockout time steps regardless of costs, and the second one consists of optimizing the logistic ratio while preserving the number of stockout to zero. For each phase, a simple first-improvement randomized descent is used. Accepting neutral moves helps us to diversify the search and then converge toward high-quality solutions. The move to apply is chosen randomly with equal probability over all moves in the pool (improvements being marginal, further tunings with non-uniform distribution have been abandoned to facilitate maintenance and evolutions).

Two kinds of moves are used: one move works on operations, the other works on shifts. The moves on operations are described in Figure 1.4). The moves on shifts can be outlined in a few words: insertion, deletion, rolling, move, swap, fusion and separation. These moves, and more generally our multiple neighborhood approach, is fully in line with the trends observed in [SÖR 08] (discovered after this work). As done for the car sequencing problem, these core moves are derived from the very generic (move an operation randomly picked from all) to the very specific (move an operation from a customer to a closest one). The latter ones allow us to speed up the convergence, while the former ones ensure diversifying the search. We can observe that no very large-scale neighborhood is employed. Roughly speaking, the neighborhood explored has a size $O(n^2)$ with n being the number of operations and shifts in the current solution, but the constant hidden by the O notation is large. Indeed, the number of moves (counting all the derivations) exceeds 50.

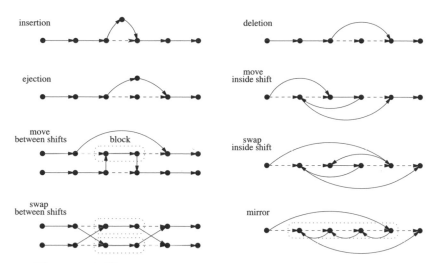

Figure 1.4. *The moves on operations. Original tours are given by straight arcs, dashed arcs are removed by the move, curved and vertical arcs are added by the move*

1.3.3. *Incremental evaluation machinery*

Playing a central role in the efficiency of the local search heuristic, only the evaluation procedure is outlined here. For each move, this procedure follows the same process. First, the modified shifts are rescheduled in order to compute new dates for its operations, checking all routing constraints. Then, the delivered or loaded quantities are recomputed for all operations impacted by the move and their inventories are updated. Finally, the new number of stockouts and new logistic ratios are computed. Roughly speaking, the objective of the scheduling routine is to build shifts with smallest costs, whereas the volume assignment tends to maximize the quantity delivered to customers. Even approximately, it leads to us minimizing the logistic ratio.

When a shift is impacted by a move (for example, an operation is inserted into the shift), the starting and ending dates of its operations must be computed anew. We can reschedule dates forward or backward. Here computing dates can be done without assigning volumes to operations, because their durations do not depend on delivered/loaded quantities. Then, the problem is: having fixed its starting date and the order of its stops, schedule the shift with the earliest ending date. Similar problems have been recently studied in [ARC 09, GOE 10, GOE 09] but the algorithms proposed (exact or approximate) runs in $O(n^2)$ or even in $O(n^3)$ time, with n being the number of operations to schedule (no more than 10 per shift). For the sake of efficiency, an $O(n)$-time algorithm has been designed to solve heuristically this shift scheduling problem. This algorithm is greedy in the sense that operations are chronologically set without backtracking. We try to minimize the unproductive time over the shift. Thereby, the main idea behind the algorithm is to take rests as late as possible during the trip and to avoid waiting time due to opening time windows of locations as much as possible. Here we try to remove waiting time by converting it into rest time, but only on the current arc, which is suboptimal (see Figure 1.5). However, we have observed that waiting time is rarely generated in practice since many trips are completed in a day or even half a day, ensuring the optimality of the algorithm in most cases.

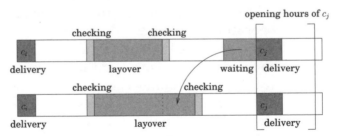

Figure 1.5. *An example with waiting time converted into rest time*

Having rescheduled modified shifts, we have to reassign quantities to impacted operations. Having fixed the dates of all operations, the problem consists of assigning volumes such that inventory constraints are respected, while maximizing the total delivered quantity over all shifts. From the theorctical view point, the present problem is not so hard once it is observed that it can be formulated as a maximum flow problem in a directed acyclic network (see Figure 1.6). This one can be solved in $O(n^3)$ time by using a classical maximum flow algorithm [COR 04], with n being the number of operations. Once again, such a time complexity is not desirable here, even if guaranteeing an optimal volume assignment. Then, an $O(n \log n)$-time greedy algorithm has been designed to solve the problem approximately. The main idea behind the algorithm is simple: having ordered operations chronologically (i.e. according to increasing starting dates), quantities are assigned to operations in this order following a greedy rule. Here we use the basic rule consisting of maximizing the quantity delivered/loaded at each operation. In graph-theoretical terms, the algorithm consists of pushing flow in the induced directed acyclic network following a topological order of the nodes, ensuring that no node is visited twice. Because the number of operations n is large (several hundreds), this algorithm remains too time-consuming, even if running in nearly linear time.

Hence, the greedy algorithm has been revisited to compute minimal reassignments. It consists of changing only the volumes on the impacted operations: the operations whose dates are modified by the move and the ones whose inventory has to be updated. This notably complicates its practical implementation. Indeed, changing the quantity delivered at an operation is delicate since increasing (respectively decreasing) the quantity may imply overflows (respectively stockouts) at future operations. Then, determining the quantity to deliver/load at each operation is not straightforward. Hence, an $O(\bar{n} \log \bar{n})$-time algorithm was designed for assigning volumes, with $\bar{n}$ being the number of impacted operations. In theory, this greedy algorithm is far from being optimal. One can construct simple networks for which the greedy algorithm fails to find an optimal assignment. However, two sufficient conditions hold for which the greedy assignment is optimal: each customer is served at most once over the planning horizon; each shift visits only one customer. These conditions are interesting because they frequently met in practice. The running time of this critical routine is shown to be *100 times faster than the full application of the greedy algorithm* ($\bar{n} = n$) and *2,000 times faster than exact algorithms*. However, the total volume delivered by the routine is close to the optimal assignment, in particular when no stockout appears: the average gap between the greedy assignment and an optimal assignment is lower than 2 %.

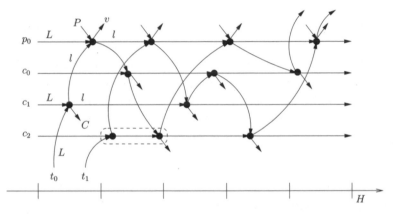

Figure 1.6. *An example of flow network for assigning volumes. Operations are represented by nodes, input flows L correspond to initial levels for each inventory (trailers t_i, customers c_i, plants p_i), input flow C (respectively P) corresponds to consumption of customer c_1 (respectively production of plant p_0) over the time steps between the current operation and the previous one, flow l correspond to inventory levels between two operations, flow v allows an overflow at plant. Flows on arcs representing inventory levels are upper bounded by the capacity of the inventory; for customers, flows are also lower bounded by safety levels. Note that if some consecutive operations appear over the same time step (like the ones which are dotted around), input flows corresponding to consumption or production are cumulated at the last operation of this time step*

The whole local search heuristic was implemented in C# programming language. The resulting program includes nearly 30,000 lines of code, whose 20 % of which are dedicated to checking the validity of all incremental data structures at each iteration (only active in debug mode). On average, our algorithm explores nearly 1 million feasible solutions within the 5 min of running time, even for large-scale instances. The average gain exceeds 20 % over urgency-based greedy solutions or even by expert planners. An extensive computational study can be found in our paper [BEN 09].

2

Local Search for 0–1 Nonlinear Programming

Mixed-integer linear programming (MILP or simply MIP) is undoubtedly the most powerful general-purpose approach to combinatorial optimization. Based on a simple and rather generic mathematical formalism, MIP offers powerful software tools to operations research (OR) practitioners to solve real-world combinatorial problems. The success of MIP [BIX 12] is so big that MIP solvers are now an indispensable tool for OR engineers and researchers. We think that this success is due to two factors: first, the simplicity of the MIP formalism (the language serving as an interface with the user), second, the ease of use of MIP "model-and-run" solvers (the user models his problem, the solver resolves it). We can observe that constraint programming (CP) now follows the road toward pure model-and-run solvers [PUG 04].

Despite the remarkable progresses made over the past 15 years [BIX 12], MIP solvers always fail to solve many of the highly combinatorial problems encountered in the practice of OR. Indeed, MIP solvers still fail to find even feasible solutions to problems inducing only thousands of binary decisions. Renault's car sequencing problem [EST 08] studied in Chapter 1 is a good example. The linear relaxation is not good enough to effectively prune the exponential branch-and-bound tree. Thus, the search provides no feasible solution after hours of computation. When MIP solvers are ineffective, practitioners generally implement hand-made local search algorithms to obtain good-quality feasible solutions quickly. However, dedicated local search approaches, even if industrialized as explained in Chapter 1, induce extra costs in development and maintenance.

2.1. The LocalSolver project

Tree search approaches like branch-and-bound are in essence designed to *prove optimality* that is different from what users first expect: *good feasible solutions quickly*. Moreover, tree search has an exponential behavior which makes it *not scalable* faced with real-world combinatorial problems inducing millions of binary decisions. The two problems addressed in Chapter 1 are some good examples of combinatorial or mixed-variable optimization problems intractable with current model-and-run solvers, in particular MIP solvers. The most striking fact about this reality can be observed in the famous and intensively studied Traveling Saleman Problem (TSP). The largest TSP instances for which the optimal solution is known counts 85,900 cities [APP 09]. The solution is first computed by local search and then proved to be optimal by branch-and-cut. While obtaining the solution takes hours using LKH – the high-end implementation of Lin-Kernighan local search by Helsgaun [HEL 00, HEL 09], it takes 136 CPU years to prove its optimality using Concorde – the branch-and-cut code by Applegate *et al.* [APP 09]. Moreover, LKH is able to provide near-optimal solutions in minutes to TSP instances with 10s of millions of cities; it holds the record for the World TSP with 1,904,711 cities.

Indeed, tree search suffers from several drawbacks in practice. When tackling highly-combinatorial problems, linear relaxation in MIP or filtering in CP are often useless but cost a lot in computational efficiency. Thus, why lose time to enumerate partial solutions? Another issue concerns the erraticism of tree search [FIS 14]: tree search is not really suited to randomly explore (without bias) a solution space. So why would an incomplete tree search (which is mostly the case in practice) be better than local search? An interesting fact is that MIP and CP solvers integrate more and more local search ingredients into their branching heuristics [LOD 13]: large neighborhood search [SHA 98, FOC 03], local branching [FIS 03, FIS 08], or relaxed induced neighborhood search [DAN 05]. Consequently, we are convinced that local search is the technique of choice to scale up, since each step (i.e. each move) can generally be performed in sublinear or even constant time. If carefully designed and implemented, the resulting algorithms converge *empirically* toward high-quality solutions in weakly polynomial time. For example, the convergence of LKH [HEL 09] toward near-optimal TSP solutions is shown to grow in linear time. Similar behaviors can be exhibited for the numerous local search heuristics implemented by our team [BEN 09, BEN 11a, EST 06, EST 08, EST 09, GAR 11, JEA 11] to solve large-scale combinatorial optimization problems arising in business and industry.

Started in 2007, the goal of the *LocalSolver* project [BEN 11b] was to offer the power of pure and direct local search to practitioners through a model-and-run solver. The objectives of this applied research project were to design a simple and general mathematical formalism suited for local search (model) and to develop an effective solver based on pure and direct local search (run). The design of the local search solver was guided by a fundamental principle according to us: the solver must at least do what an expert would do facing the problem (as exposed in section 1.1). Since 2012, LocalSolver[1] is commercialized by Innovation 24, subsidiary of Bouygues Group, in partnership with Aix-Marseille Université and the French National Center for Scientific Research (CNRS–LIF Marseille), but its use remains free for the academic community. Having reviewed the related works in the literature, the modeling formalism associated with the current version of LocalSolver [3.1] is presented. Then, the main ideas on which LocalSolver relies are outlined. Finally, some computational results are provided demonstrating the effectiveness of LocalSolver compared to state-of-the-art model-and-run solvers.

---

1 http://www.localsolver.com.

2.2. State-of-the-art

Leveraging the power of local search into software tools which are easy to use by OR practitioners is a quest which has started at the beginning of the 1990s. Most proposals made to offer tools or reusable components for local search programmers take the form of a framework handling the top layer of the algorithm, namely metaheuristics (see for example [CAH 04, DI 03]). In this case, moves and associated incremental algorithms are implemented by the user, while the framework is responsible for applying the selected parameterized metaheuristic. However, designing moves and implementing incremental evaluation algorithms represent the largest part of the work (and of the resulting source code). As mentioned in Chapter 1, these two layers consume about 30% and 60% of the development times respectively. Moreover, the algorithmic layer dedicated to the evaluation of moves is particularly difficult to engineer, because it requires both an expertise in algorithms and a dexterity in computer programming. Hence, these frameworks do not address the hardest issues of local search algorithms engineering. Two frameworks aim to answer to these needs: Comet Constraint-Based Local Search (CBLS) [VAN 05] (and its ancestor Localizer [MIC 00]) and iOpt [VOU 01]. These tools allow an automatic evaluation of moves, but the implementation of these moves remains the responsibility of the user. Note that a generic swap-based tabu search procedure [DYN 10] is available in Comet CBLS 2.1, which can be used for tackling directly integer models.

State-of-the-art MIP or CP solvers include more and more heuristic features, some of which are related to local search. Berthold [BER 06] provides an extensive survey of primal heuristics for MIP. Among them, we can cite large neighborhood search [FOC 03, SHA 98] used in CP, as well as local branching [FIS 03, FIS 08] or relaxed induced neighborhood search [DAN 05] in mixed-integer programming. Nevertheless, all these works consist of integrating high-level local search ingredients into the tree search paradigm, whereas the actual power of local search relies on fast incremental computations made possible by small modifications of the incumbent solution.

Some attempts have been made to use pure and direct local search approaches in discrete mathematical programming. The most famous ones have been introduced by researchers from the artificial intelligence community. Indeed, some of the best provers for Satisfiability Testing (SAT) or pseudo-Boolean programming rely on stochastic local search (see for example Walksat [SEL 96] and WSAT(OIP) [WAL 99]). Some attempts have been made in binary programming [CON 92, NON 98] or in integer programming [ABR 99, RAN 01]. In all cases, the main difficulty encountered by the authors is that modifying some binary variables randomly frequently leads to infeasible solutions and that recovering feasibility is difficult and long, causing a very slow convergence toward good-quality solutions or even feasible solutions. This issue is highlighted by the fact that local search works very well in solving unconstrained binary programming, in particular unconstrained binary quadratic programming [LÜ 09].

Ultimately, to the best of our knowledge, no effective and widely used model-and-run solver exploiting the power of pure and direct local search is currently available for tackling large-scale real-life combinatorial optimization problems. Developing such a solver was initially the goal of the LocalSolver project [BEN 11b].

2.3. Enriching modeling standards

Modeling is a crucial part of the job in mathematical optimization. The user of math programming software has to model his problem in a suitable way in the hope of finding an effective automatic resolution by the software. In this way, the mathematical formalism which is offered to the user is decisive. From the beginning of the use of mathematical optimization in business and industry, there has been a need for simple and clear algebraic modeling languages to ease the communication with optimization solvers. In a recent historical paper, Fourer [FOU 12] describes the evolution from matrix generators to modeling languages. Nevertheless, a bottleneck remains. Modeling languages allow a high-level description of mathematical optimization problems, but this is partially lost when passed to the solver. Indeed, mathematical programming solvers still only accept matrix representations as standard input. We can observe that such a low-level representation has several drawbacks for the resolution process itself.

For the sake of clarity, practitioners profusely use intermediate variables in their models. Now in matrix representations, decision variables are not distinguished from intermediate variables, the ones whose value can be deduced from the values of decision variables. Then, all the assignments induced by the declaration of these intermediate variables are set as constraints when passed to the solver. Many primal heuristics in mixed-integer programming suffer from this loss of information [BER 06]. The prior attempts to tackle pseudo-Boolean or integer programs [ABR 99, CON 92, NON 98, RAN 01] by local search faced the same problem. Note that modern MIP solvers extensively use heuristic preprocessing procedures to recover a part of this lost information [LOD 13]. Another drawback of matrix representation arises in nonlinear optimization. Specifying a nonlinear model as a matrix is not convenient for users. Expressions built with classical mathematical functions like the division or the power are difficult to set in such a format. Making the interface with nonlinear solvers complicated, this issue appears as an obstacle to their use and thus to their development. According to ourselves, more expressiveness is better for users as well as for solvers. Inspired by the state-of-the-art modeling systems [FOU 12], we propose a new data representation for mathematical optimization solvers, as well as a new mathematical modeling/scripting language to support this one. This data representation, called LocalSolver Model (LSM), and the associated scripting language, called LocalSolver Programming language (LSP), are implemented in LocalSolver [BEN 11b].

2.3.1. *LocalSolver modeling formalism*

The modeling formalism supported by LocalSolver is close to the classical 0-1 integer programming formalism. However, it is enriched by common mathematical operators that makes it easy to use by OR practitioners. The LSM representation of a mathematical optimization instance corresponds to its algebraic expression tree. More precisely, the subjacent data structure is a directed acyclic graph (DAG). Its root nodes are the decision variables of the model. Each inner node corresponds to an intermediate variable, whose value is computed by applying a predefined mathematical operator on its parent variables in the DAG. These inner nodes are related to so-called one-way constraints or invariants in CP-oriented frameworks like iOpt [VOU 01] or Comet [VAN 05] (or its ancestor Localizer [MIC 00]). Then, each variable (also called expression) can be tagged as constrained, minimized, or maximized. Only Boolean expressions can actually be constrained to be true. In this way, a solution is a complete instantiation of the decisions such that all constraints in the model are satisfied.

Following the LSM format, a mathematical optimization model simply consists of declaring the decision variables, building some expressions based on these decisions and then tagging some expressions as constraints or objectives. Note that the user shares no information about the way which the model is stored or even solved internally. For example a toy problem is described in Figure 2.1. The statement `bool()` creates a Boolean decision variable, i.e. a decision variable whose value is false or true. Boolean variables are treated as integers, with the convention false=0 and true=1. Then, the keyword `<-` is used to define intermediate variables `sx` and `sy` that can be Boolean or integer. The keyword `constraint` prefixes each constraint definition. In the same way, the keyword `minimize` prefixes the objective of the program. In the current version of LocalSolver [3.1], only Boolean decisions are managed but extending the grammar to integer or continuous decision variables is straightforward. Expressions can be built upon decisions or other expressions (without recursion) by using given arithmetic, logical, relational or conditional operators like `sum`, `prod`, `min`, `max`, `div`, `mod`, `sub`, `abs`, `log`, `exp`, `pow`, `cos`, `sin`, `tan`, `and`, `or`, `xor`, `not`, `eq`, `neq`, `geq`, `leq`, `gt`, `lt`, `iif`, and others. In summary, the LSM format is based on a functional syntax, with no limitation on the nesting of expressions. Some mathematical operators only apply to a certain number of arguments or to a certain type of expressions. For instance, the `not` operator takes only one argument whose type must be Boolean, whereas `sum` or `and` can take an arbitrary number of arguments. The conditional operator `iif` takes exactly three arguments, the first one being necessarily Boolean.

Any Boolean expression can be constrained to be true by prefixing the expression with `constraint`. An instantiation of decision variables is valid if and only if all constraints take value 1, coding for satisfied. As explained in Chapter 1, hard constraints have to be carefully considered when modeling real-world problems. Many of the constraints expressed by users are unlikely to be satisfied in real-life: these ones have to be considered as primary objectives. The LSM formalism offers a feature making it easy to do so. The objectives can be defined using the modifier `minimize` or `maximize`. Any expression can be used as objective. If several objectives are defined, they are interpreted as a lexicographic objective function. The lexicographic ordering is induced by the order in which the objectives are declared. For instance, in car sequencing with paint colors, when the goal is to minimize violations on ratio constraints and then the number of paint color changes, the objective function can be directly specified as: `minimize ratio_violations;` and `minimize color_changes`. This feature allows avoiding the classical modeling workaround where a big coefficient is used to simulate the lexicographic order: `minimize 1000 ratio_violations + color_changes`. Note that the number of objectives is not limited and can have different directions (minimization or maximization).

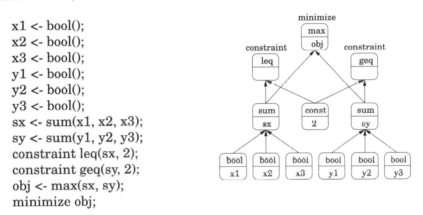

```
x1 <- bool();
x2 <- bool();
x3 <- bool();
y1 <- bool();
y2 <- bool();
y3 <- bool();
sx <- sum(x1, x2, x3);
sy <- sum(y1, y2, y3);
constraint leq(sx, 2);
constraint geq(sy, 2);
obj <- max(sx, sy);
minimize obj;
```

Figure 2.1. *The directed acyclic graph (on the right) induced by a toy LSM model (on the left). For each node, the type (resp. name) of the node is given above (resp. below)*

For the sake of simplicity and readability, LSM was presented as a file format (i.e. as a grammar). But LSM must be viewed as an interface between the user and the solver. Then, it can be implemented as an application programming interface for any computing framework (for example, C or XML). Such interfaces are currently provided as libraries for

C++, Java and .NET languages in the LocalSolver package.

2.3.2. *LocalSolver programming language*

The mathematical expressiveness offered by the LSM formalism is richer than the classical matrix representation required in input of mathematical programming solvers. Even if LSM can be viewed as a language, it is not convenient to be used as a modeling language. Indeed, LSM offers no programming feature. Then, we have embedded LSM into an innovative programming language for mathematical optimization, namely LSP. The current version of the LSP language is dedicated to rapid prototyping: it embeds modeling features into a lightweight scripting language.

In summary, the LSP language is interpreted, strongly typed but dynamic, with an implicit declaration of variables. It offers many built-in variables and functions. The mathematical built-in functions can be used for both modeling or programming. For instance, c <- a * b means that an expression c is declared corresponding to the product of modeling variables a and b. On the other hand, c = a * b means that the product of programming variables a and b is assigned to c. Usual mathematical symbols like + or <= can be used as shortcuts in an infix way. An innovative compact looping syntax [i in 0..n] can be used to iterate over a set of variables or expressions. A short LSP program is described below to illustrate the main features of the language. More examples can be found in the LocalSolver example tour, directly available from the Web.[2]

```
/* multiobjective_knapsack.lsp */

function input() {
```

---

2 http://www.localsolver.com/exampletour.html.

```
nbItems = 8; sackBound = 102;
weights = {2, 20, 20, 30, 40, 30, 60, 10};
values = {15, 100, 90, 60, 40, 15, 10, 1};

function model() {
  // 0-1 decisions
  x[0..nbItems-1] <- bool();

  // weight constraint
  sackWeight <- sum[i in 0..nbItems-1](weights[i] * x[i]);
  constraint sackWeight <= sackBound;

  // maximize value
  sackValue <- sum[i in 0..nbItems-1](values[i] * x[i]);
  maximize sackValue;

  // secondary objective: minimize the product of
    minimum and maximum values
  sackMinValue <- min[i in 0..nbItems-1](x[i] ? values[i] : 1000);
  sackMaxValue <- max[i in 0..nbItems-1](x[i] ? values[i] : 0);
  sackProduct <- sackMinValue * sackMaxValue;
  minimize sackProduct;
}

function param() {
  lsTimeLimit = 60; lsNbThreads = 4;
}
```

2.4. The core algorithmic ideas

In this section, we outline the two ingredients which are critical to the effectiveness of our approach. These naturally follow the methodology exposed previously: multiple randomized small-neighborhood moves as well as a highly-optimized incremental evaluation machinery. Our main innovation lies in the design of local search moves working on abstract combinatorial structures, far beyond the basic "flips" used in SAT solvers.

2.4.1. *Effective local search moves*

As suggested in introducing the LocalSolver project, we wish that our solver autonomously performs the moves that an experimented practitioner would have designed to solve the problem, and ultimately some moves he would certainly not implement: complex small-neighborhood moves (like 3,4,5-opt moves for the traveling salesman problem) or even compound moves. The main characteristic of such moves is to maintain the feasibility of the incumbent solution, or at least the feasibility of the constraints inducing the essence of its combinatorial structure. Indeed, the main conclusions of the few attempts to tackle 0-1 programs by local search [ABR 99, CON 92, NON 98, RAN 01] are related to this issue: simple flips or even k-flips are ineffective because recovering feasibility takes too much time. Maintaining feasibility means performing moves ensuring that the resulting solution remains in the solution space. Thus, performing moves allowing us to search on hypersurfaces (for instance, on the classical hyperplane induced by the linear equality constraint $\sum_i A_i x_i = B$) is crucial for effectiveness and efficiency. Of course, the more constrained the problem is, the smaller the solution space is, and the more difficult the search will be. As explained in Chapter 1, hardly-constrained problems encountered in the real world mostly result from a bad understanding of the user needs or from bad modeling practices, yielding the risk of "no solution found" answers to the end-users. Our idea to maintain feasibility while performing a move on the 0-1 solution vector is inspired from ejection chain techniques [REG 02] or destroy and repair techniques [PER 04b]: *having flipped a Boolean decision, repair violated constraints by flipping other Boolean decisions.* Finding the latter Boolean decisions can be done by exploiting the hypergraph induced by decisions (as vertices) and constraints (as edges). Figure 2.2 illustrates such a move, inducing a cycle along six Boolean variables while satisfying the constraints involving these six decisions.

To understand the effect of such moves, let us consider the car sequencing problem [EST 06, EST 08] introduced in Chapter 1. This problem can be modeled as an assignment problem by defining for each car i and position p a Boolean decision $x_{i,p}$. A basic move for this model consists of exchanging the positions of two vehicles. Exchanging the positions p and q of two cars i and j corresponds to flipping the 4 decisions $x_{i,p}$, $x_{i,q}$, $x_{j,q}$, $x_{j,p}$ that preserves the feasibility of the 4 partition constraints where these variables appear. In fact, paths (or cycles) of alternating flips along the constraints correspond to classical k-move or k-exchange neighborhoods for assignment, partitioning, packing, or covering problems.

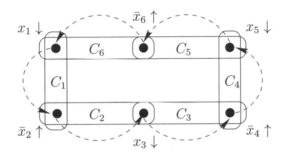

Figure 2.2. *A cyclic move involving six Boolean variables* x_1, x_3, x_5 *(whose current value is 1) and* $\bar{x}_2$, $\bar{x}_4$, $\bar{x}_6$ *(whose current value is 0), and six constrained sums* $C_1, \ldots, C_6$. *Each variable belongs to two sums (for example,* x_1 *belongs to* C_1 *and* C_6). *Now,* x_1, x_3, x_5 *are decreased (↓) while* $\bar{x}_2$, $\bar{x}_4$, $\bar{x}_6$ *are increased (↑). This move preserves the values of the sums, and thus the feasibility of the constraints*

Many variants of the chain or cycle described above can be derived. These variants can be specific to some combinatorial structures (i.e. to some constraint hypergraphs) – with higher probabilities of success, to speed up the convergence of the search – or more generic – with lower probabilities of success, but favoring the diversification of the search. In the same way, they can induce small neighborhoods or larger ones, leading to more or less efficient incremental evaluations. For example, flipping more than one decision when repairing a constraint induces more complex walks along the constraint network, whose trace is then related to subgraphs in the constraint hypergraph. In packing problems, such moves allow ejecting two objects of size 1 while adding an object of size 2 in the same set. At each iteration of the search, the move to apply is selected randomly following a distribution dynamically adapted along the search. Moves often leading to infeasible solutions tend to be abandoned. However, moves with larger acceptance or improvement rates are more frequently attempted.

2.4.2. *Incremental evaluation machinery*

The practical power of local search relies on the efficiency of the moves. When only impacting the solution vector locally (i.e. modifying only a few of its coordinates), these moves can be quickly evaluated through incremental computations. Incremental computation belongs to the folklore of computer science and algorithm engineering. To our knowledge, the first mathematical optimization frameworks involving an automatic incremental evaluation are Localizer [MIC 00] (the ancestor of Comet [VAN 05]) and iOpt [VOU 01]. Based on a modeling formalism similar to LocalSolver modeling formalism, the incremental evaluation relies on invariants induced by mathematical operators. Although we claim no novelty for this mechanism, we emphasize the main specificities of our implementation in LocalSolver.

The fast evaluation of moves is obtained by exploiting the invariants induced by each type of node (i.e. operators) during the propagation [MIC 00]. A breadth-first search propagation of the modifications is performed along the DAG, guaranteeing that each node is evaluated once at most. Following a classical observer pattern, the propagation is reduced to impacted nodes: a node is said to be impacted if some of its parents have been modified. For example, consider the node $z \leftarrow a < b$ with a current value equal to true. This will not be impacted if a is decreased or b increased. Then, each node of the DAG implements the following methods: init, eval, commit, rollback. The method init is responsible for the initialization of the value of the node according to (the values of) its parents, before starting the search. The specific data structures attached to the node, used for speeding up its incremental evaluation, are also initialized by this method. Having applied a move on decision variables, the `eval` method is called to re-evaluate the value of a node incrementally, when this one is impacted during the DAG propagation. Then, if the move is accepted (according to the search strategy), the `commit` method is called up on each modified node for validating the changes implied by the move. Otherwise, the move is rejected, and the `rollback` method is used instead.

The `eval` method takes in input the list of modified parents, i.e. the parent nodes whose current value has changed. For a linear operator like `sum`, the evaluation is easy: if k terms of the sum are modified, then its new value is computed in $O(k)$ time. But for nonlinear operators, significant accelerations can be obtained in practice. For example, consider the node $z \leftarrow \text{or}(a_1, \ldots, a_k)$ with M, the list of modified a_i's and T the list of a_i's whose current value is true. Thus, one can observe that if $|M| \neq |T|$, then the new value of z is necessarily true, leading to a constant-time evaluation. Indeed, if $|M| < |T|$, then at least one parent remains with a value equal to true; otherwise, there exists at least one parent whose value is modified from false to true. Our implementation is focused on the *empirical* time complexity, and not only on the worst-case time complexity. Constant factors do matter: fine algorithmic and code optimizations improve speed of evaluation by several orders of magnitude. To our knowledge, the property mentioned above to maintain the `or` operator is not employed in Comet or iOpt systems. In the same way, in Localizer [MIC 00], the `min` operator is classically maintained in $O(\log k)$ time with k, the number of operands using a binary heap. In LocalSolver, we distinguish two cases. If the minimum value among the modified operands is lower than or equal to the current value of the `min` operator, or if one support remains unmodified, then the evaluation is optimally done in $O(|M|)$ time with $|M|$, the number of modified values. Otherwise, the evaluation is performed in $O(k)$ time. In practice, the former case is by far the most frequent and the number of modified operands is small (i.e. $|M| = O(1)$), ensuring an amortized constant-time evaluation.

2.5. Benchmarks

LocalSolver was tested on a benchmark mixing academic and industrial problems. We insist on the fact that our purpose is not to achieve state-of-the-art results for all the tested problems. The main goal of LocalSolver is to obtain, used as a black box, good-quality solutions quickly, in particular when tree search solvers fail to find any solution. Thus, LocalSolver is compared to existing model-and-run solvers, here the state-of-the-art MIP solver Gurobi[3], on a standard computer equipped with the operating system Windows 7 x64 and a chip Intel Core i7-820QM (4 cores, 1.73 GHz, 6 GB RAM, 8 MB cache). As expected, the main conclusion is that LocalSolver outperforms tree search solvers by several orders of magnitude when large-scale combinatorial optimization problems are addressed. Older results can be found in our paper [BEN 11b] where our early prototype LocalSolver 1.1 is compared to IBM ILOG CPLEX 12.2[4].

2.5.1. *Car sequencing*

Here we outline the results obtained in the car sequencing problem, addressed in Chapter 1. LocalSolver and Gurobi are

---

3 http://www.gurobi.com.

4 http://www-01.ibm.com/software/integration/optimization/cplex-optimizer.

launched with their default parameter settings. Note that the results obtained by model-and-run CP or SAT solvers are not mentioned because they are not competitive (see for example results presented in [PER 04a, PER 04b]). For each solver, we use a standard model adapted to the formalism of the solver. For both solvers, the assignment of cars to positions is modeled with Boolean variables and the violations in each ratio constraint are summed (see [EST 06] for details). Sample results are presented for 5 instances in Table 2.1: 10–93 (100 cars, 5 options, 25 classes), 200–01 (200 cars, 5 options, 25 classes), 300–01 (300 cars, 5 options, 25 classes), 400–01 (400 cars, 5 options, 25 classes), 500–08 (500 cars, 8 options, 20 classes). The first 4 instances are available in CSPLib[5]; the fifth comes from a benchmark generated by [PER 04b]. The line "state-of-the-art" corresponds to the state-of-the-art results obtained by our local search algorithm, described in [EST 06]. The results presented in the table have been obtained with a fixed time limit of 10, 60 and 600 s respectively; the corresponding LSP file is given in the LocalSolver Example Tour[6]. The cost of the best solution found is given (the symbol X is used if no solution has been obtained within the time limit, the symbol * is added to indicate that the solution found was *proved* optimal). In summary, we can observe that LocalSolver outperforms Gurobi as the scale of instances grows.

More interesting are the results obtained in the real-world version integrating the constraints and objectives of the paint workshop proposed by Renault as subject of the ROADEF 2005 Challenge[7] which was discussed in section 1.2. Table 2.2 contains sample results for four instances: I1 = 022-EP-ENP-RAF-S22-J1 (540 cars, 9 options, 14 colors), I2 = 023-EP-RAF-ENP-S49-J2 (1260 cars, 12 options, 13 colors),

---

5 http://www.csplib.org.

6 http://www.localsolver.com/exampletour.html?file=car_sequencing.zip.

7 http://challenge.roadef.org/2005/en.

I3 = 024-EP-RAF-ENP-S49-J2 (1319 cars, 18 options, 15 colors), I4 = 025-EP-ENP-RAF-S49-J1 (996 cars, 20 options, 20 colors). The state-of-the art corresponds to the local search heuristic described in section 1.2, which won the challenge [EST 08, SOL 08]. Note that the engineering of this dedicated algorithm required nearly 80 working days of the authors. In contrast, Gurobi finds no feasible solution after several hours of computation for instances I2, I3, I4. After one hour of running time, Gurobi obtains a solution whose cost is 194,161 for I1, which is far from LocalSolver's result within 5 min only. For instance I3, the resulting LocalSolver model contains 516,936 expressions whose 374,596 are binary decisions (less than 50 MB of RAM are required for the execution). Localsolver explores nearly 1 million *feasible* solutions per minute. According to its results, LocalSolver would have been ranked among the top competitors of the ROADEF 2005 Challenge. In particular, LocalSolver outperforms the dedicated variable neighborhood search by [PRA 08] mixing classical moves and large neighborhood search by MIP.

Time limit: 10 s	10–93	200–01	300–01	400–01	500–08
Gurobi 5.5	140	274	X	429	513
LocalSolver 3.1	**6**	8	9	11	24
LocalSolver 4.0 beta	8	**5**	**8**	**10**	**19**
Time limit: 60 s	10–93	200–01	300–01	400–01	500–08
Gurobi 5.5	**3**	66	1	356	513
LocalSolver 3.1	6	**3**	**3**	7	10
LocalSolver 4.0 beta	6	4	**3**	**5**	**6**
Time limit: 600 s	10–93	200–01	300–01	400–01	500–08
Gurobi 5.5	**3**	2	**0***	1	20
LocalSolver 3.1	6	2	1	2	4
LocalSolver 4.0 beta	4	**0***	**0***	2	**0***
State-of-the-art	3	0*	0*	1	0*
Binary decisions	500	1000	1500	2000	4000

Table 2.1. *Sample results for the academic car sequencing problem*

Time limit: 600 s	I1	I2	I3	I4
Gurobi 5.5	3,027,839	X	X	X
LocalSolver 3.1	3,120	**217,058**	11,423,006	166,632
LocalSolver 4.0 beta	**3,114**	240,075	**382,010**	**160,572**
State-of-the-art	3,109	192,066	337,006	160,407
Binary decisions	44,184	259,560	374,596	278,880

Table 2.2. *Sample results for Renault's car sequencing problem*

2.5.2. *Machine scheduling*

Another striking result was recently obtained in the context of the ROADEF/EURO 2012 Challenge[8]. This real-world problem, posed by Google, consists of reassigning processes to machines while respecting different kinds of constraints (resources, mutual exclusions, etc.). The aim of this challenge is to improve the usage of a set of machines. A machine has several resources, like CPU and RAM for example, and runs processes which consume these resources. Initially each process is assigned to a machine. In order to improve the machine usage, processes can be moved from one machine to another. Possible moves are limited by hard constraints, for example resource capacity constraints, and have a cost. A solution to this problem is a new process-machine assignment which satisfies all hard constraints and minimizes a given objective cost.

Using a 100-line mathematical model[9], LocalSolver was able to qualify for the final round of the Challenge, ranking 25th out of 82 participating teams. LocalSolver is able to tackle the 10 instances from set A (until 100,000 decisions) within 5 min on a standard computer with 4 GB RAM. For all instances except the toy A1-1 (400 binary decisions), no model-and-run solver is able to provide a feasible solution within the time limit, to our knowledge. LocalSolver is able to solve some of the ultra-large instances from set B (from

---

8 http://challenge.roadef.org/2012/en.
9 http://www.localsolver.com/exampletour.html?file=google_machine_reassignment.zip.

500,000 to 250 million 0–1 decisions). It depends on the amount of RAM available on the computer. With 4 GB of RAM, we can tackle B1, B2. With 40 GB of RAM, you can tackle all instances except B7, B9, B10. In the latter case, we can notably attack instance B4 with 1 million decisions, 114 million expressions, 1.6 million constraints. The results obtained within 5 min on our standard computer with 6 GB RAM are detailed in Table 2.3.

Instances	Expressions	Decisions	Constraints	LocalSolver 3.1	LocalSolver 4.0 beta	State-of-the-art
A1-1	6,020	400	503	44,306,501	44,306,501	44,306,501
A1-2	1,812,044	100,000	100,595	797,041,378	791,337,884	777,532,896
A1-3	1,423,438	100,000	26,097	583,007,622	583,006,420	583,005,717
A1-4	753,404	50,000	9,913	295,785,797	277,578,924	252,728,589
A1-5	229,213	12,000	13,905	727,578,409	727,578,309	727,578,309
A2-1	1,415,324	100,000	102,300	8,176,319	4,513,099	198
A2-2	3,769,381	100,000	19,770	1,328,470,442	1,216,918,411	816,523,983
A2-3	3,843,977	100,000	20,213	1,738,822,512	1,566,648,617	1,306,868,761
A2-4	1,537,771	50,000	13,373	2,309,678,761	2,054,256,551	1,681,353,943
A2-5	1,556,017	50,000	13,260	601,850,679	551,397,584	336,170,182
B1	10,165,011	500,000	284,155	4,436,929,040	4,352,763,543	3,339,186,879
B2	8,117,249	500,000	273,799	1,475,082,345	1,412,787,354	1,015,553,800

Table 2.3. *Results on Google's machine reassignment with 6 GB RAM (300 s)*

2.5.3. *Quadratic assignment problem*

The quadratic assignment problem (QAP) [BUR 97] is a classic of the operations research literature. The problem involves n facilities and n locations. For each pair of locations, a distance is specified and for each pair of facilities a weight or flow is specified (for example, the amount of supplies transported between the two facilities). The problem consists of assigning all facilities to different locations with the goal of minimizing the sum of the distances multiplied by the corresponding flows. Intuitively, the objective encourages factories with high flows between each other to be placed close together. The problem statement is similar to the assignment problem, except that the cost function is composed of quadratic terms instead of linear terms.

In Table 2.4, we present the results obtained by LocalSolver 3.1 using a basic model[10], within 5 min of running time. The state-of-the-art corresponds to the best result known today, as referenced in the webpage[11] maintained by P. Hahn. Since mixed-integer (linear or quadratic) programming solvers are not competitive in QAP, we have omitted their results (no feasible solution is found within the time limit on the majority of instances).

2.5.4. MIPLIB 2010

We recently developed a tool to translate an MIP model (LP or MPS format) into a LocalSolver model (LSM format). Since the LocalSolver formalism is richer than the MIP formalism, this transformation is heuristic, trying to distinguish decision variables from intermediate variables and to recover some nonlinear expressions from matrix-oriented linear constraints. This tool allows us to translate and solve successfully a number of the hardest and largest MIP instances of MIPLIB 2010,[12] the well-known benchmark for MIP solvers. The results are given in Table 2.5 below. This experiment shows that LocalSolver is able to provide quality solutions to large-scale problems which are not suitably modeled and structured for LocalSolver.

To conclude, we invite the readers to have a look to the LocalSolver Example Tour[13] to find more results obtained using LocalSolver in difficult problems. In particular, in the recent versions 3.0 and 3.1 of LocalSolver, some moves dedicated to combinatorial structures encountered in scheduling or routing problems have been designed. This allows us to obtain good-quality results in short running

---

10 http://www.localsolver.com/exampletour.html?file=qap.zip.

11 http://www.seas.upenn.edu/qaplib.

12 http://miplib.zib.de.

13 http://www.localsolver.com/exampletour.html.

times on traveling salesman problems[14] and vehicle routing problems.[15]

Instances	n	Decisions	Expressions	LocalSolver 3.1	State-of-the-art	Gap
esc32a	32	1,024	124,299	136	130	5 %
esc32b	32	1,024	180,872	188	168	12 %
esc32c	32	1,024	219,153	642	642	0 %
esc32d	32	1,024	150,922	200	200	0 %
esc32e	32	1,024	11,148	2	2	0 %
esc32g	32	1,024	16,138	6	6	0 %
esc32h	32	1,024	235,791	444	438	1 %
kra30a	30	900	288,166	92,130	88,900	4 %
kra30b	30	900	288,166	93,020	91,420	2 %
kra32	32	1,024	328,558	94,440	88,700	6 %
lipa30a	30	900	732,736	13,399	13,178	2 %
lipa30b	30	900	731,258	177,255	151,426	17 %
lipa40a	40	1,600	2,374,581	31,998	31,538	1 %
lipa40b	40	1,600	2,368,797	565,314	476,581	19 %
lipa50a	50	2,500	5,885,226	62,859	62,093	1 %
lipa50b	50	2,500	5,876,130	1,431,681	1,210,244	18 %
nug30	30	900	510,877	6,238	6,124	2 %
sko42	42	1,764	2,078,709	16,282	15,812	3 %
sko49	49	2,401	3,817,588	24,146	23,386	3 %
ste36a	36	1,296	435,141	10,488	9,526	10 %
ste36b	36	1,296	435,628	18,066	15,852	14 %
ste36c	36	1,296	435,822	8,612,782	8,239,110	5 %
tai30a	30	900	745,196	1,914,966	1,818,146	5 %
tai30b	30	900	484,316	638,762,469	637,117,113	0 %
tai35a	35	1,225	1,384,849	2,515,194	2,422,002	4 %
tai35b	35	1,225	737,819	287,227,702	283,315,445	1 %
tai40a	40	1,600	2,382,379	3,284,344	3,139,370	5 %
tai40b	40	1,600	1,341,640	689,131,580	637,250,948	8 %
tai50a	50	2,500	5,905,491	5,230,902	4,938,796	6 %
tai50b	50	2,500	2,911,505	481,156,669	458,821,517	5 %
tho30	30	900	379,599	153,286	149,936	2 %
tho40	40	1,600	976,311	249,326	240,516	4 %
wil50	50	2,500	5,387,864	49,526	48,816	1 %
average						5 %

Table 2.4. *Results on the QAPLIB (300 s)*

---

14 http://www.localsolver.com/exampletour.html?file=tsp.zip.

15 http://www.localsolver.com/exampletour.html?file=vrp.zip.

Instances	Status	Variables	LocalSolver 3.1	Gurobi 5.5	Optimum
opm2-z10-s2	hard	6,250	-25,719	-19,601	-33,826
opm2-z11-s8	hard	8,019	-33,028	-21,661	-43,485
opm2-z12-s14	hard	10,800	-46,957	-11,994	-64,291
opm2-z12-s7	hard	10,800	-46,034	-12,375	-65,514
pb6	hard	462	-62	-62	-63
queens-30	hard	900	-38	-36	-40
dc11	open	37,297	11,100,000	21,300,000	Unknown
ds-big	open	6,020	9,844	62,520	Unknown
ex1010-pi	open	25,200	249	251	Unknown
ivu06-big	open	1,812,044	479	9,416	Unknown
ivu52	open	1,423,438	4,907	16,880	Unknown
mining	open	753,404	-65,720,600	902,969,000	Unknown
ns-1853823	open	213,440	2,820,000	4,670,000	Unknown
pb-simp-nonunif	open	23,848	90	140	Unknown
ramos3	open	2,187	223	274	Unknown
rmine14	open	32,205	-3,469	-170	Unknown
rmine21	open	162,547	-3,657	-184	Unknown
rmine25	open	326,599	-3,052	-161	Unknown
siena1	open	13,741	256,620,000	315,186,152	Unknown
sts405	open	405	342	342	Unknown
sts729	open	709	648	648	Unknown

Table 2.5. *Results on some of the hardest instances of the MIPLIB 2010 (300 s)*

3

Toward an Optimization Solver Based on Neighborhood Search

In Chapter 2, we have shown that 0-1 nonlinear programming can be efficiently tackled by local search. Exploiting pure and direct local search allows us to tackle combinatorial problems, which are out of scope of the state-of-the-art tree search solvers (MIP or CP). This was made possible by designing fast, scalable local moves tending to maintain the search in feasible regions. The core idea behind these local moves is to modify the current value of some decisions while repairing violated constraints. We conclude this book by outlining our current work on LocalSolver and more generally by presenting the roadmap of the LocalSolver project toward a generalized, all-in-one, hybrid mathematical programming solver based on neighborhood search.

3.1. Using neighborhood search as global search strategy

As explained previously, pure tree search approaches suffer from several drawbacks, which makes them ineffective for large-scale optimization. Let us cite Fischetti and Monaci [FIS 14] about tree search: "Our working hypothesis is that erraticism is in fact just a consequence of the exponential nature of tree search, that acts as a chaotic amplifier, so it is largely unavoidable." This explains the reason why today tree search solvers (mixed-integer programming (MIP), constraint programming (CP), satisfiability (SAT)) integrate more and more heuristic ingredients related to local search [DAN 05, FIS 03, FIS 08, FOC 03, SHA 98]. In modern solvers, tree search is mainly used to perform large neighborhood exploration around some promising solutions (see for example [FIS 03] or [SHA 98]). Since relaxation or propagation are expensive to compute, particularly for large-scale problems, variable-fixing heuristics [BER 06] are intensively used at each node of the tree search to find feasible integer solutions.

We propose a general-purpose optimization solver founded on a radically different architecture. Instead of embedding local search ingredients into tree search, we propose to use neighborhood search as a global search strategy. Nevertheless, neighborhood search does not mean restricting the search to small neighborhoods and abandoning tree search. Very large-scale neighborhoods, namely neighborhoods of exponential size, can be explored through tree search or specific algorithms (see our papers [EST 06, EST 08] for example). This way of searching follows the methodology exposed in section 1.1. The type and the size of the neighborhood explored at each iteration are dynamically adapted along the search. As shown in Chapter 2, small-neighborhood moves – mainly running in $O(1)$ time – are critical for the velocity of the search: they speed up the convergence toward good-quality feasible solutions and allows us to scale when facing problems with millions of variables. Then, if exploring small neighborhoods fails to improve the best incumbent or to diversify the search (which occurs when the search is trapped into a local optimum or confined to a hardly constrained subspace), then larger neighborhoods can be explored to escape the current solution. As explained in section 1.1, this can be done by using compound moves or even large-neighborhood moves based on tree search [ROT 07] or specific algorithms [AHU 02]. Such moves are more expensive in running time, so they have to be used parsimoniously, ideally only when it is necessary. Note that when the number of decisions is not so large, some large neighborhood moves based on tree search can handle all decisions of the problem: in this case, the neighborhood explored corresponds to the entire solution space, making the search complete.

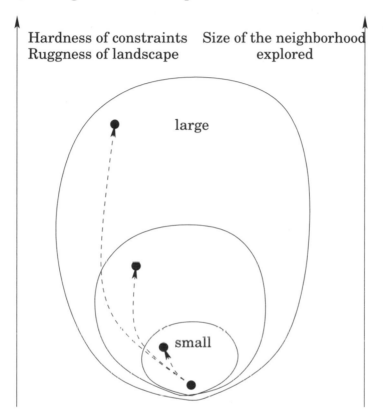

Figure 3.1. *Enlarging or retracting the neighborhood to explore, during the search*

An important ingredient is the randomization of the whole search process, in particular the exploration of the neighborhoods. Even if small neighborhood moves are sufficient to progress, some large neighborhood moves can also be called to diversify the search, with a low probability. Moves are applied randomly following a distribution evolving during the search. This distribution is changed based on the acceptance and improvement rates of each kind of move and of the time complexity of these moves. Then, the top-layer heuristic which pilots the search allows several levels of diversification in addition to the moves. A strategy mixing simulated annealing with thresholds [AAR 03] is used to escape from local optima for small neighborhoods. In case of very chaotic landscapes, the search can be restarted from feasible points (reheating) or from infeasible points (restart). Finally, the search is multithreaded. It consists of running different searches in parallel and synchronizing them regularly.

In this way, the neighborhood search strategy implemented in LocalSolver generalizes and unifies many known ideas and concepts: variable neighborhood search [HAN 08], multiple neighborhood search [SÖR 08] and autonomous search [HAM 12]. Coupling simulated annealing, multiple neighborhood search and the hyper-heuristic learning mechanism, the search strategy recently proposed by Bai *et al.* [BAI 12, BAI 13] is close to the one implemented in LocalSolver. Note that this kind of local/global search strategy is heavily used in global optimization to practically solve non-convex continuous or mixed-variable problems (see [LIB 06] for more details).

3.2. Extension to continuous and mixed optimization

Local search is a technique which is actually used in continuous optimization, under another name: *direct search*. The technique was introduced in the 1960s for unconstrained nonlinear programming (with continuous decisions) through the "other simplex method", namely the Nelder-Mead simplex algorithm [NEL 65, WRI 12]. Direct search [KOL 03] refers to *derivative-free or zeroth-order methods*, in contrast to first-order methods requiring the computation of gradients like quasi-Newton methods, or second-order methods requiring the computation of the Hessian matrix like Newton methods (see [MIN 07] for more details). Reading the recent survey by Kolda *et al.* [KOL 03], the parallel between local search methods in combinatorial optimization and direct search methods in continuous optimization is striking: the apparent conceptual simplicity of the approach, the notion of "moves" applied at each iteration of the search (see [KOL 03]), the fast evaluation of each iteration directly based on the objective, as well as the lack of mathematical analysis explaining its practical efficiency. Surprisingly, the similarity does not stop at technicalities: "Mathematicians hate it because you cannot prove convergence; engineers seem to love it because it often works" commented John Nelder himself [WRI 12].

However, similar to local search in combinatorial optimization, direct search appears to be limited in tackling constrained problems, even if some progress has been made recently [KOL 03]. We are currently working on *unifying local search for combinatorial optimization and direct search for continuous optimization*. In particular, we have adapted the local search moves described in Chapter 2, to handle continuous decisions. The ideas behind these local continuous (or even mixed-variable) moves remain the same: we tend to maintain the feasibility of the move by repairing violated constraints, we exploit incremental calculations to evaluate the move quickly. In summary, we are working to make LocalSolver able to tackle *large-scale mixed-variable non-convex optimization problems* involving both 0-1 and continuous decisions. In the same way as for combinatorial optimization, some moves exploring larger neighborhoods will be designed based on first-order (linear) or second-order (convex) approximations, as done in interior point methods or sequential linear/quadratic programming for nonlinear programming [LEY 10].

More generally, our goal with this research line is *to promote the use of direct / local search, and more generally of approximate computing techniques [NAI 08a, NAI 08b], as primary techniques to search and optimize efficiently in any kind of solution space, in particular to cope with very large-scale, highly non-convex problems encountered in real-world optimization.* This approach is radically different from the mainstream in mathematical programming. Despite some attempts, such as the use of pattern search or variable neighborhood search in global optimization [KOL 03, LIB 06, LIB 11], most of the works in combinatorial or continuous optimization concentrated on the design of sophisticated techniques providing *guarantees* in terms of convergence toward optimal solutions or locally optimal solutions. Such mathematical guarantees have a price: these techniques involve heavy computations at each step, leading to slow or even impractical algorithms for large-scale real-world optimization. For example, many state-of-the-art optimization algorithms follow a best-improvement approach, in the sense that they search *at each step* the next best iteration (in particular, the best direction to follow). For example, at each iteration of the simplex algorithm for linear programming, the best swap of columns (one column entering the basis and another column leaving it) requires us to invert the basis matrix and to compute the reduced costs for all non-basic variables, basically involving $O(m^2 + nm)$ multiplications with n (respectively, m) the number of variables (respectively, constraints) [COR 04]. In convex programming, while the number of iterations of many interior point algorithms is reduced to roughly $O(\sqrt{n})$ in the worst case, the practical complexity of each iteration is still much more expensive than one of the simplex algorithm's. Indeed, the computation of the Newton direction requires $O(n^3)$ time with n the number of variables [BEN 01]. In combinatorial optimization, algorithms for maximum flow or maximum matching computes at each iteration the best augmenting path, requiring a $O(m)$-time breadth-first search with m the number of edges in the graph [COR 04]. In integer programming, tree search approaches rely on the computation of a lower bound at each node, based on the *exact* linear relaxation reinforced by cut generation. Table 3.1 gives a more explicit comparison of the practical efficiency of some of the search paradigms described above.

Our idea is to use direct local search to lower the practical time complexity of one iteration, averaged and amortized over the entire search, in any kind of solution space. Indeed, if a lightweight move suffices to make a step in the right direction (i.e. to improve the incumbent), why not perform it? The idea is to use heavier moves exploring larger neighborhoods (possibly changing more coordinates of the solution vector) to diversify or intensify the search, in particular when the lightweight moves become ineffective. As explained above, this can be made adaptively and randomly throughout the search, leading to two major advantages in practice. First, it speeds up the convergence toward good-quality feasible solutions. Then, it allows us to scale when facing ultra-large instances, as encountered today in the practice of optimization.

	Iterations per minute	Speedup factor
LP interior point	≈ 10	-
LP simplex	$\approx 10,000$	$\times 1,000$
Small-neighborhood search	$\approx 10,000,000$	$\times 1,000,000$

Table 3.1. *Comparison of the "velocity" of different search techniques to tackle a real-life continuous linear problem (LP) involving nearly 100,000 variables and 1 million nonzeros*

3.3. Separating the computation of solutions and bounds

According to ourselves, finding feasible solutions (i.e. computing upper bounds) and proving optimality (i.e. computing lower bounds) are different tasks, requiring different approaches. Modern MIP solvers use primal feasibility heuristics [BER 06] to quickly produce feasible solutions *before* starting the tree search. Then, these two tasks are handled *separately* in LocalSolver. On the one hand, feasible solutions are searched and optimized through a local/global search approach, as described in the section 2.2. On the other hand, lower bounds are improved through relaxation and inference techniques embedded in a divide-and-conquer scheme. Information is exchanged between the two calculations to enhance both. Our goal is to obtain exponential-inverse convergence patterns for both computations, even when facing very large-scale problems.

Relaxation techniques take their roots in the field of mathematical programming. The idea is to relax the original problem such that the relaxed problem can be solved efficiently, to obtain a lower bound of the optimal solution to the original problem. So far, (continuous) linear problems have been the ones we practically solve better today. This explains the success of mixed-integer *linear* programming solvers, relying on the computation of the linear relaxation by the simplex algorithm. A line of research was initiated 20 years ago to take advantage of convex relaxations, in particular semidefinite relaxations [VAN 96], for combinatorial optimization [MAL 13] or more generally mixed-variable non-convex optimization [LIB 06]. On the other hand, inference and constraint propagation techniques have been developed in the field of artificial intelligence. Inference techniques are the heart of SAT solvers (see [HAM 08] for a survey on conflict learning). Extending inference techniques to problems which have decisions over arbitrary domains (and not only Boolean ones), constraint propagation is the heart of CP solvers (see [BES 06] for a survey). Many ideas developed in the SAT and CP fields can be integrated in a general-purpose mathematical optimization solver like LocalSolver. It is a good way to improve the optimality gap when relaxation techniques are failing, which is generally the case when the problem is highly combinatorial [BER 09]. As pointed in [HAM 08], resolution techniques in SAT are related to cutting plane generation techniques in MIP.

We have started to integrate both relaxation and inference techniques in LocalSolver to compute lower bounds. In the previous Chapter 2, some results presented in Table 2.1 related to the car sequencing problem show the ability of LocalSolver to prove optimality. First, a dual linear relaxation of the input model is automatically generated and heuristically solved by the local/global search techniques presented in the previous section. Using a dual relaxation instead of a primal one, we allow ourselves to exploit an iterative improvement solution approach, since every dual feasible solution induces a lower bound. The idea is to follow the same scheme as the one advocated for computing feasible solutions of the original problem: using approximate resolution techniques to speed up the bounding and to be able to scale when necessary. Similar ideas have recently been introduced through the so called primal-dual variable neighborhood search [HAN 07, HAN 09]. In the spirit of the line of research initiated by Malick and Roupin [MAL 13], the next step will be to reinforce the linear bounds by using dual convex relaxations. On the other hand, we have integrated inference techniques relying on identifying richer discrete structures (global constraints). This bounding process – relaxation and propagation – will be embedded in a divide-and-conquer process (that is, a branching process dealing with discrete and continuous domains), defining an iterative improvement scheme to reduce the optimality gap. To go further, resolution techniques (cutting plane generation or conflict learning) have to be integrated in this process to tighten relaxation and propagation, in particular for combinatorial optimization. To deal with continuous domains, we plan to apply interval propagation and filtering techniques combining interval analysis and constraint programming features (see [CHA 09, JAU 01] for details).

3.4. A   new-generation,   hybrid   mathematical programming solver

In this final section, we outline the target architecture of LocalSolver over the long term. Our vision of mathematical programming and then the future of LocalSolver can be summarized by citing the conclusion of a prospective paper by John N. Hooker [HOO 07] written in 2007 about the future of constraint programming and operations research: "Since modeling is the master and computation the servant, no computational method should presume to have its own solver. This means there should be no CP solvers, no MIP solvers, and no SAT solvers. All of these techniques should be available in a single system to solve the model at hand. They should seamlessly combine to exploit problem structure. Exact methods should evolve gracefully into inexact and heuristic methods as the problem scales up."

Following the previous discussions, the target architecture of LocalSolver is drawn in Figure 3.2. Through this architecture, *we unify heuristic and exact optimization approaches in two ways*: first by adopting a *generalized (i.e. multiple, variable, adaptive) neighborhood search approach* – from small neighborhoods explored in a heuristic fashion to large neighborhoods explored in an exact fashion – then by *dissociating the search and the optimization of feasible solutions (search into the primal solution space) from the computation of lower bounds aiming at proving optimality or infeasibility (search into the dual solution space)*. This way of unifying mathematical optimization techniques extend the recent ideas independently suggested by Hooker in a forthcoming paper [HOO 13], while being consistent with his (and our) vision of the future of mathematical programming described above.

Planned for the end of 2013, the next version 4.0 will be a first step toward this new-generation mathematical programming solver for *large-scale mixed-variable non-convex optimization*, hybridizing all appropriate optimization techniques: local and direct search techniques, constraint programming and satisfiability techniques, mixed-integer and nonlinear programming techniques, etc. Indeed, the next versions will progressively offer several important features from both functional and technical points of view: small-neighborhood moves to optimize over continuous or mixed decisions; exploration of large, exponential-size neighborhoods over 0-1 or mixed decisions using tree search techniques (for example, rounding heuristics based on linear relaxation); exploration of large neighborhoods over continuous decisions by revisiting successive linear programming techniques for nonlinear programming (based on a simplex algorithm); computation of lower bounds combining constraint propagation and dual linear relaxation.

As an example, we provide some preliminary results on the unit commitment problem [PAD 04] as addressed in Benoist [BEN 07], which is a celebrated mixed-decision nonlinear (convex quadratic) optimization. The unit commitment problem is an optimization problem used to determine the operation schedule of the generating units at every hour interval with varying loads under different constraints and environments. This problem is traditionally solved using Lagrangian relaxation approaches [PAD 04]. In Table 3.2, we give the results obtained after 5 min of running time using a straightforward LocalSolver model (in version 4.0 beta). The state-of-the-art results presented in this table have been obtained by a heuristic based on Lagrangian relaxation [BEN 07].

In the long term, we plan to add *integer decisions and set operators* in the LocalSolver formalism to make the modeling of routing and scheduling problems easier (and the resolution more efficient, in particular about space complexity). Nevertheless, mixing this richer formalism with the classical

0-1 decision formalism is delicate for users (see for example the proposals by Hooker *et al.* [HOO 09, YUN 10] on this topic). Indeed, integers can be used as quantitative variables or as indexers for set operators.

Instances	Time steps	Units	Decisions	Expressions	LocalSolver 4.0 beta	State of the art	Gap
ucp0	8	4	64	850	75,037	74,988	0,07 %
ucp3	24	10	480	5,946	572,558	563,719	1,57 %
ucp4	24	20	960	11,709	1,160,470	1,122,042	3,42 %
ucp5	24	40	1,920	23,230	2,403,470	2,237,824	7,40 %
ucp6	24	60	2,880	34,748	3,544,590	3,355,191	5,64 %
ucp7	24	80	3,840	46,270	4,765,150	4,470,455	6,59 %
ucp8	24	100	4,800	57,788	5,984,610	5,587,788	7,10 %

Table 3.2. *Results on a unit commitment problem*

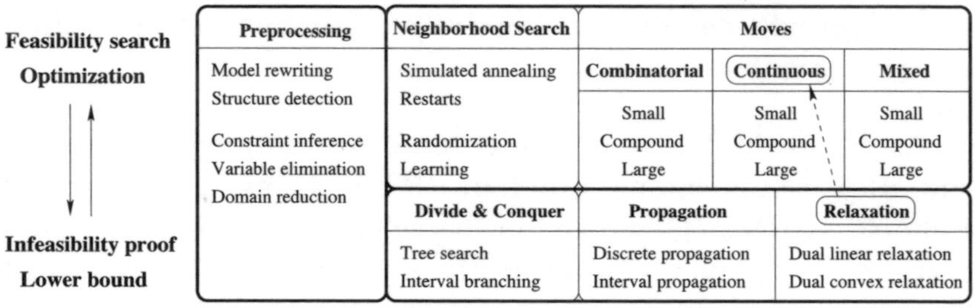

Figure 3.2. *Target architecture of LocalSolver*

Bibliography

[AAR 03] AARTS E., LENSTRA J.K., *Local Search in Combinatorial Optimization*, 2nd ed., Princeton University Press, 2003.

[ABR 99] ABRAMSON D., RANDALL M., "A simulated annealing code for general integer linear programs", *Annals of Operations Research*, vol. 86, pp. 3–21, 1999.

[AHU 02] AHUJA R.K., ERGUN Ö., ORLIN J.B., *et al.*, "A survey of very large-scale neighborhood search techniques", *Discrete Applied Mathematics*, vol. 123, pp. 75–102, 2002.

[APP 09] APPLEGATE D.L., BIXBY R.E., CHVÁTAL V., *et al.*, "Certification of an optimal TSP tour through 85,900 cities", *Operations Research Letters*, vol. 37, pp. 11–15, 2009.

[ARC 09] ARCHETTI C., SAVELSBERGH M., "The trip scheduling problem", *Transportation Science*, vol. 43, no. 4, pp. 417–431, 2009.

[BAI 12] BAI R., BLAZEWICZ J., BURKE E.K., *et al.*, "A simulated annealing hyper-heuristic methodology for flexible decision support", *4OR*, vol. 10, no. 1, pp. 43–66, 2012.

[BAI 13] BAI R., VAN WOENSEL T., KENDALL G., et al., "A new model and a hyper-heuristic approach for two-dimensional shelf space allocation", *4OR*, vol. 11, no. 1, pp. 31–55, 2013.

[BAR 01] BARNETT L., "Netcrawling: optimal evolutionary search with neutral networks", *Proceedings of the 2001 IEEE Congress on Evolutionary Computation*, IEEE, pp. 30–37, 2001.

[BAZ 06] BAZARAA M.S., SHERALI H.D., SHETTY C.M., *Nonlinear Programming: Theory and Algorithms*, John Wiley & Sons, 2006.

[BEL 83] BELL W., DALBERTO L., FISHER M., et al., "Improving the distribution of industrial gases with an on-line computerized routing and scheduling optimizer", *Interfaces*, vol. 13, no. 6, pp. 4–23, 1983.

[BEL 13] BELOTTI P., KIRCHES C., LEYFFER S., et al., "Mixed-integer nonlinear optimization", *Acta Numerica*, vol. 22, pp. 1–131, 2013.

[BEN 01] BEN-TAL A., NEMIROVSKI A., *Lectures on Modern Convex Optimization*, MPS-SIAM Series on Optimization, SIAM, 2001.

[BEN 07] BENOIST T., "Décomposition combinatoire et applications industrielles", *Collection Programmation par Constraintes*, Hermes Science, Lavoisier, 2007.

[BEN 09] BENOIST T., ESTELLON B., GARDI F., et al., "Randomized local search for real-life inventory routing", *Transportation Science*, vol. 45, no. 3, pp. 381–398, 2009.

[BEN 11a] BENOIST T., GARDI F., JEANJEAN A., "Lessons learned from 15 years of operations research for French TV channel TF1", *Interfaces*, vol. 42, no. 6, pp. 577–584, 2011.

[BEN 11b] BENOIST T., ESTELLON B., GARDI F., *et al.*, "LocalSolver 1.x: a black-box local-search solver for 0-1 programming", *4OR*, vol. 9, no. 3, pp. 299-316, 2011.

[BER 06] BERTHOLD T., Primal heuristics for mixed integer programs, Diploma Thesis, Technical University of Berlin, Konrad-Zuse-Zentrum für Informationstechnik Berlin, 2006.

[BER 09] BERTHOLD T., HEINZ S., PFETSCH M.E., "Nonlinear pseudo-Boolean optimization: relaxation or propagation?", *Proceedings of SAT 2009*, LNCS 5584, Springer, pp. 441–446, 2009.

[BES 06] BESSIÈRE C., Constraint propagation, Technical Report LIRMM 06020, CNRS/University of Montpellier, France, 2006.

[BIX 12] BIXBY R.E., "A brief history of linear and mixed-integer programming computation", *Optimization Stories, 21st ISMP Berlin 2012*, Documenta Mathematica, pp. 107–121, 2012.

[BON 00] BONNANS J.F., GILBERT J.C., LEMARÉCHAL C., *et al.*, *Numerical Optimization: Theoretical and Practical Aspects*, Springer, 2000.

[BUR 97] BURKARD R.E., KARISCH S.E., RENDL F., "QAPLIB – a quadratic assignment problem library", *Journal of Global Optimization*, vol. 10, no. 4, pp. 391–403, 1997.

[BUR 12] BURER S., LETCHFORD A.N., "Non-convex mixed-integer nonlinear programming: a survey", *Surveys in Operations Research and Management Science*, vol. 17, no. 2, pp. 97–106, 2012.

[BUS 11] BUSSIECK M.R., VIGERSKE S., "MINLP solver software", *Wiley Encyclopedia of Operations Research and Management Science*, John Wiley & Sons, pp. 95–113, 2011.

[CAH 04] CAHON S., MELAB N., TALBI E-G., "ParadisEO: a framework for the reusable design of parallel and distributed metaheuristics", *Journal of Heuristics*, vol. 10, no. 3, pp. 357–380, 2004.

[CAM 98] CAMPBELL A., CLARKE L., KLEYWEGT A., *et al.*, "The inventory routing problem", *Fleet Management and Logistics*, Kluwer Academic Publishers, pp. 95–113, 1998.

[CAM 02] CAMPBELL A., CLARKE L., SAVELSBERGH M., "Inventory routing in practice", *The Vehicle Routing Problem*, SIAM Monographs on Discrete Mathematics and Applications, vol. 9, SIAM, pp. 309–330, 2002.

[CAM 04a] CAMPBELL A., SAVELSBERGH M., "A decomposition approach for the inventory-routing problem", *Transportation Science* vol. 38, no. 4, pp. 488–502, 2004.

[CAM 04b] CAMPBELL A., SAVELSBERGH M., "Delivery volume optimization", *Transportation Science* vol. 38, no. 2, pp. 210–223, 2004.

[CAM 04c] CAMPBELL A., SAVELSBERGH M., "Efficient insertion heuristics for vehicle routing and scheduling problems", *Transportation Science*, vol. 38, no. 3, pp. 369–378, 2004.

[CHA 09] CHABERT G., JAULIN L., "Contractor programming", *Artificial Intelligence*, vol. 173, no. 11, pp. 1079–1100, 2009.

[CON 92] CONNOLLY D., "General purpose simulated annealing", *Journal of the Operational Research Society*, vol. 43, pp. 495–505, 1992.

[COO 12] COOK W., "Markowitz and Manne + Eastman + Land and Doig = Branch and Bound", *Optimization Stories, 21st ISMP Berlin 2012*, Documenta Mathematica, pp. 227–238, 2012.

[COR 04] CORMEN T., LEISERSON C., RIVEST R., *et al.*, *Introduction à l'Algorithmique* 2nd ed., Dunod, 2004.

[DAM 11] D'AMBROSIO C., LODI A., "Mixed integer nonlinear programming tools: a practical overview", *4OR*, vol. 9, no. 4, pp. 329–349, 2011.

[DAN 05] DANNA E., ROTHBERG E., LE PAPE C., "Exploring relaxation induced neighborhoods to improve MIP solutions", *Mathematical Programming Series A*, vol. 102, no. 1, pp. 71–90, 2005.

[DI 03] DI GASPERO L., SCHAERF A., "EasyLocal++: an object-oriented framework for flexible design of local search algorithms", *Software – Practice & Experience*, vol. 33, no. 8, pp. 733–765, 2003.

[DYN 10] DYNADEC DECISION TECHNOLOGIES, Comet 2.1 Tutorial, 2010.

[EST 06] ESTELLON B., GARDI F., NOUIOUA K., "Large neighborhood improvements for solving car sequencing problems", *RAIRO Operations Research*, vol. 40, no. 4, pp. 355–379, 2006.

[EST 08] ESTELLON B., GARDI F., NOUIOUA K., "Two local search approaches for solving real-life car sequencing problems", *European Journal of Operational Research*, vol. 191, no. 3, pp. 928–944, 2008.

[EST 09] ESTELLON B., GARDI F., NOUIOUA K., "High-performance local search for task scheduling with human resource allocation", *Proceedings of SLS 2009*, LNCS 5752, Springer, pp. 1–15, 2009.

[EST 13] ESTELLON B., GARDI F., "Car sequencing is NP–hard: a short proof", *Journal of the Operational Research Society*, vol. 64, no. 10, pp.1503–1504, 2013.

[FOU 12] FOURER R., "On the evolution of optimization modeling systems", *Optimization Stories, 21st ISMP Berlin 2012*, Documenta Mathematica, pp. 377–388, 2012.

[FIS 03] FISCHETTI M., LODI A., "Local branching", *Mathematical Programming Series B*, vol. 98, nos. 1–3, pp. 23–47, 2003.

[FIS 08] FISCHETTI M., LODI A., "Repairing MIP infeasibility through local branching", *Computers and Operations Research*, vol. 35, no. 5, pp. 1436–1445, 2008.

[FOC 03] FOCACCI F., LABURTHE F., LODI A., "Local search and constraint programming", *Handbook of Metaheuristics*, International Series in Operations Research and Management Science, Kluwer Academic Publishers, vol. 57, pp. 369–403, 2003.

[FIS 14] FISCHETTI M., MONACI M., "Exploiting erraticism in search", *Operations Research*, vol. 62, no. 1, pp. 114–122. 2014.

[GAR 11] GARDI F., NOUIOUA K., "Local search for mixed-integer nonlinear optimization: a methodology and an application", *Proceedings of EvoCOP 2011*, LNCS 6622, Springer, pp. 167–178, 2011.

[GAR 12] GARDI F., "High-performance local search for TV media planning on TF1", *EURO 2012*, Vilnius, 2012.

[GLO 86] GLOVER F., "Future paths for integer programming and links to artificial intelligence", *Computers and Operations Research*, vol. 13, no. 5, pp. 533–549, 1986.

[GLO 03] GLOVER F.W., KOCHENBERGER G.A., *Handbook of Metaheuristics*, International Series in Operations Research and Management Science, Kluwer Academic Publishers, vol. 57, 2003.

[GOE 10] GOEL A., "Truck driver scheduling in the European Union", *Transportation Science*, vol. 44, no. 4, pp. 429–441, 2010.

[GOE 09] GOEL A., KOK L., "Truck driver scheduling in the United States", *Transportation Science*, vol. 43, no. 3, pp. 317–326, 2009.

[GOT 03] GOTTLIEB J., PUCHTA M., SOLNON C., "A study of greedy, local search and ant colony optimization approaches for car sequencing problems", *Proceedings of EvoWorkshops 2003*, LNCS 2611, Springer, pp. 246–257, 2003.

[GRA 05] GRAVEL M., GAGNÉ C., PRICE W.L., "Review and comparison of three methods for the solution of the car sequencing problem", *Journal of the Operational Research Society*, vol. 56, pp. 1287–1295, 2005.

[HAM 08] HAMADI Y., JABBOUR S., SAIS L., "Learning from conflicts in propositional satisfiability", *4OR*, vol. 10, no. 1, pp. 15–32, 2008.

[HAM 12] HAMADI Y., MONFROY E., SAUBION F., *Autonomous Search*, Springer, 2012.

[HAN 08] HANSEN P., MLADENOVI N., MORENO PÉREZ J.A., "Variable neighborhood search: methods and applications", *4OR*, vol. 6, no. 4, pp. 319–360, 2008.

[HAN 07] HANSEN P., BRINBERG J., UROEVIC D., *et al.*, "Primal-dual variable neighborhood search for the simple plant-location problem", *INFORMS Journal on Computing*, vol. 19, no. 4, pp. 552–564, 2007.

[HAN 09] HANSEN P., BRINBERG J., UROEVIC D., *et al.*, "Solving large p-median clustering problems by primal-dual variable neighborhood search", *Data Mining and Knowledge Discovery*, vol. 19, no. 3, pp. 351–375, 2009.

[HEL 00] HELSGAUN K., "An effective implementation of the Lin-Kernighan traveling salesman heuristic", *European Journal of Operational Research*, vol. 126, no. 1, pp. 106–130, 2000.

[HEL 09] HELSGAUN K., "General k-opt submoves for the Lin-Kernighan TSP heuristic", *Mathematical Programming Computation*, vol. 1, pp. 119–163, 2009.

[HOO 07] HOOKER J.N., "Good and bad futures for constraint programming (and operations research)", *Constraint Programming Letters*, vol. 1, pp. 21–32, 2007.

[HOO 09] HOOKER J.N., "Hybrid modeling", *Hybrid Optimization: The Ten Years of CPAIOR*, Springer, pp. 11–62, available at http://onlinelibrary.wiley.com/doi/10.1111/itor.12020/full, 2009.

[HOO 13] HOOKER J.N., "Toward unification of exact and heuristic optimization methods", *International Transactions in Operations Research*, in press., available at http://onlinelibrary.wiley.com/doi/10.1111/itor.12020/full, 2013.

[JAU 01] JAULIN L., KIEFFER M., DIDRIT O., *et al.*, *Applied Interval Analysis with Examples in Parameter and State Estimation, Robust Control and Robotics*, Springer, 2001.

[JEA 11] JEANJEAN A., Recherche locale pour l'optimisation en variables mixtes: méthodologie et applications industrielles, PhD Thesis, École Polytechnique, Palaiseau, France, 2011.

[JON 10] JONES D.F., TAMIZ M., *Practical Goal Programming*, International Series in Operations Research and Management Science, Springer, vol. 141, 2010.

[KIS 04] KIS T., "On the complexity of the car sequencing problem", *Operations Research Letters*, vol. 32, pp. 331–335, 2004.

[KOL 03] KOLDA T.G., LEWIS R.M., TORCZON V., "Optimization by direct search: new perspectives on some classical and modern methods", *SIAM Review*, vol. 45, no. 3, pp. 385–482, 2003.

[LEY 10] LEYFFER S., MAHAJAN A., "Nonlinear constrained optimization: methods and software", Preprint ANL/MCS-P1729-0310, Argonne National Laboratory, IL, 2010.

[LIB 06] LIBERTI L., MACULAN N., *Global Optimization: From Theory to Implementation*, Series in Nonconvex Optimization and Its Applications, Springer, vol. 84, 2006.

[LIB 11] LIBERTI L., MLADENOVI N., NANNICINI G., "A recipe for finding good solutions to MINLPs", *Mathematical Programming Computation*, vol. 3, no. 4, pp. 349–390, 2011.

[LOD 13] LODI A., "The heuristic (dark) side of MIP solvers", *Hybrid Metaheuristics*, Studies in Computational Intelligence, Springer, vol. 434, pp. 273–284, 2013.

[LØK 07] LØKKETANGEN A., "The importance of being careful", *Proceedings of SLS 2007*, LNCS 4638, Springer, pp. 1–15, 2007.

[LÜ 09] LÜ Z., GLOVER F., HAO J.-K., "Neighborhood combination for unconstrained binary quadratic problems", *Proceedings of MIC 2009*, Springer, pp. 49–61, 2009.

[MAL 13] MALICK J., ROUPIN F., "On the bridge between combinatorial optimization and nonlinear optimization: new semidefinite bounds for 0–1 quadratic problems leading to quasi-Newton methods", *Mathematical Programming Series B*, vol. 140, no. 1, pp. 99–124, 2013.

[MIC 00] MICHEL L., VAN HENTENRYCK P., "Localizer", *Constraints*, vol. 5, no. 1–2, pp. 43–84, 2000.

[MIN 07] MINOUX M., *Programmation Mathématique: Théorie et Algorithmes*, 2nd ed., Éditions Tec & Doc, Lavoisier, 2007.

[MOR 02a] MORET B.M.E., "Towards a discipline of experimental algorithmics", *Data Structures, Near Neighbor Searches, and Methodology: 5th and 6th DIMACS Implementation Challenges*, DIMACS Monographs, AMS, vol. 59, pp. 197–213, 2002.

[MOR 02b] MORET B.M.E., BADER D.A., WARNOW T., "High-performance algorithm engineering for computational phylogenetics", *Journal of Supercomputing*, vol. 22, no. 1, pp. 99–111, 2002.

[MOR 01] MORET B.M.E., SHAPIRO H.D., "Algorithms and experiments: the new (and old) methodology", *Journal of Universal Computer Science*, vol. 7, no. 5, pp. 434–446, 2001.

[NAI 08a] NAIR R., "Approximate computing", *Symposium on Computing Challenges 2008*, Ithaca, NY, 2008.

[NAI 08b] NAIR R., PRENER D.A., "Computing, approximately", *Wild and Crazy Ideas VI, ASPLOS 2008*, Seattle, WA, 2008.

[NEL 65] NELDER J.A., MEAD R., "A simplex method for function minimization", *Computer Journal*, vol. 7, pp. 308–313, 1965.

[NOC 06] NOCEDAL J., WRIGHT S.J., *Numerical Optimization*, Springer Series in Operations Research, 2nd ed., Springer, 2006.

[NON 98] NONOBE K., IBARAKI T., "A tabu search approach to the constraint satisfaction problem as a general problem solver", *European Journal of Operational Research*, vol. 106, nos. 2–3, pp. 599–623, 1998.

[PAD 04] PADHY N.P., "Unit commitment – a bibliographical survey", *IEEE Transactions on Power Systems*, vol. 19, no. 2, pp. 1196–1205, 2004.

[PUG 04] PUGET J.-F., "Constraint programming next challenge: simplicity of use", *Proceedings of CP 2004*, LNCS 3258, Springer, pp. 5–8, 2004.

[PEL 07] PELLEGRINI P., BIRATTARI M., "Implementation effort and performance", *Proceedings of SLS 2007*, LNCS 4638, Springer, pp. 31–45, 2007.

[PER 04a] PERRON L., SHAW P., "Combining forces to solve the car sequencing problem", *Proceedings of CPAIOR 2004*, LNCS 3011, Springer, pp. 225–239, 2004.

[PER 04b] PERRON L., SHAW P., FURNON V., "Propagation guided large neighborhood search", *Proceedings of CP 2004*, LNCS 3258, Springer, pp. 468–481, 2004.

[PIS 10] PISINGER D., ROPKE S., "Large neighborhood search", *Handbook of Metaheuristics*, International Series in Operations Research & Management Science, Springer, vol. 146, pp. 399–419, 2010.

[PRA 08] PRANDTSTETTER M., RAIDL G.R., "An integer linear programming approach and a hybrid variable neighborhood search for the car sequencing problem", *European Journal of Operational Research*, vol. 191, no. 3, pp. 1004–1022, 2008.

[PUC 02] PUCHTA M., GOTTLIEB J., "Solving car sequencing problems by local optimization", *Proceedings of EvoWorkshops 2002*, LNCS 2279, Springer, pp. 132–142, 2002.

[RAM 96] RAMALINGAM G., *Bounded Incremental Computation*, Lecture Notes in Computer Science, Springer, vol. 1089, 1996.

[RAN 01] RANDALL M., ABRAMSON D., "A general meta-heuristic based solver for combinatorial optimization problems", *Combinatorial Optimisation and Applications*, vol. 20, pp. 185–210, 2001.

[REG 02] REGO C., GLOVER F., "Local search and metaheuristics", *The Traveling Salesman Problem and Its Variations*, Kluwer Academic Publishers, pp. 105–109, 2002.

[REI 02] REIDYS C.M., STADLER C.M., "Combinatorial landscapes", *SIAM Review*, vol. 44, no. 1, pp. 3–54, 2002.

[ROS 92] ROSENBLUM D.S., "Towards a method of programming with assertions", *Proceedings of the 14th International Conference on Software Engineering (ICSE 1992)*, ACM, pp. 92–104, 1992.

[ROT 07] ROTHBERG E., "An evolutionary algorithm for polishing mixed integer programming solutions", *INFORMS Journal on Computing*, vol. 19, no. 4, pp. 534–541, 2007.

[SAV 07] SAVELSBERGH M., SONG J.-H., "Inventory routing with continuous moves", *Computers and Operations Research*, vol. 34, no. 6, pp. 1744–1763, 2007.

[SAV 08] SAVELSBERGH M., SONG J.-H., "An optimization algorithm for the inventory routing with continuous moves", *Computers and Operations Research*, vol. 35, no. 7, pp. 2266–2282, 2008.

[SCH 00] SCHRIMPFA G., SCHNEIDERB J., STAMM-WILBRANDTA H., *et al.*, "Record breaking optimization results using the ruin and recreate principle", *Journal of Computational Physics*, vol. 159, no. 2, pp. 139–171, 2000.

[SEL 92] SELMAN B., LEVESQUE H.J., MITCHELL D., "A new method for solving hard satisfiability problems", *Proceedings of AAAI 1992*, AAAI, pp. 440–446, 1992.

[SEL 96] SELMAN B., KAUTZ H., COHEN B., "Local search strategies for satisfiability testing", *Cliques, Coloring, and Satisfiability: 2nd DIMACS Implementation Challenge*, DIMACS Series in Discrete Mathematics and Theoretical Computer Science, AMS, vol 26, 1996.

[SHA 98] SHAW P., "Using constraint programming and local search methods to solve vehicle routing problems", *Proceedings of CP 1998*, LNCS 1520, Springer, pp. 417–431, 1998.

[SOL 00] SOLNON C., "Solving permutation constraint satisfaction problems with artificial ants", *Proceedings of ECAI 2000*, IOS, pp. 118–122, 2000.

[SOL 08] SOLNON C., CUNG V.-D., NGUYEN A., *et al.*, "The car sequencing problem: overview of state-of-the-art methods and industrial case-study of the ROADEF'2005 challenge problem", *European Journal of Operational Research*, vol. 191, no. 3, pp. 912–927, 2008.

[SÖR 08] SÖRENSEN K., SEVAUX M., SCHITTEKAT P., "'Multiple neighbourhood' search in commercial VRP packages: evolving towards self-adaptive methods", *Adaptive and Multilevel Metaheuristics*, Studies in Computational Intelligence, Springer, vol. 136, pp. 239–253, 2008.

[SÖR 12] SÖRENSEN K., "Metaheuristics: the metaphor exposed", *EURO 2012 Tutorials*, Vilnius, 2012.

[SPI 04] SPIELMAN D.A., TENG S.-H., "Smoothed analysis of algorithms: why the simplex algorithm usually takes polynomial time", *Journal of the ACM*, vol. 51, no. 3, pp. 385–463, 2004.

[VAN 96] VANDENBERGHE L., BOYD S., "Semidefinite programming", *SIAM Review*, vol. 38, no. 1, pp. 49–95, 1996.

[VAN 05] VAN HENTENRYCK P., MICHEL L., *Constraint-based Local Search*, MIT, 2005.

[VOU 01] VOUDOURIS C., DORNE R., LESAINT D., *et al.*, "iOpt: a software toolkit for heuristic search methods", *Proceedings of CP 2001*, LNCS 2239, pp. 716–730, 2001.

[WAL 99] WALSER J., *Integer Optimization by Local Search: A Domain-independent Approach*, Lecture Notes in Articial Intelligence, Springer, vol. 1637, 1999.

[WRI 04] WRIGHT M.H., "The interior-point revolution in optimization: history, recent developments, and lasting consequences", *Bulletin of the American Mathematical Society*, vol. 42, no. 1, pp. 39–56, 2004.

[WRI 12] WRIGHT M.H., "Nelder, Mead, and the other simplex method", *Optimization Stories, 21st ISMP Berlin 2012*, Documenta Mathematica, pp. 271–276, 2012.

[YUN 10] YUNES T., ARON I., HOOKER J.N., "An integrated solver for optimization problems", *Operations Research*, vol. 58, pp. 342–356, 2010.

[ZHA 03] ZHANG L., MALIK S., "Cache performance of SAT solvers: a case study for efficient implementation of algorithms", *Proceedings of SAT 2003*, LNCS 2919, Springer, pp. 287–298, 2003.

List of Figures and Tables

Index